Table of Contents

Introduction 5

Chapter 1: The history of The Ninja Air Fryer 6

Chapter 2: Ninja Air Fryer Techniques 10

Chapter 3: Ninja Air Fryer Cooking Advantages 14

Chapter 4: Ninja Air Fryer Maintenance 17

Chapter 5: Breakfast Recipes 21

    Crispy Breakfast Potatoes 21
    Fluffy Blueberry Pancakes 22
    Veggie Breakfast Burritos 23
    Banana-Nut Oatmeal Muffins 24
    Spinach and Feta Breakfast Quesadillas 25
    Greek Yogurt Parfait 26
    Avocado Toast with Poached Eggs 27
    Cinnamon Sugar French Toast Sticks 28
    Breakfast Burrito Dish 29
    Healthy Fruit Smoothie 30
    Breakfast Stuffed Bell Peppers 31
    Apple Cinnamon Breakfast Quinoa 32
    Sausage and Egg Breakfast Burritos 33
    Chocolate Banana Protein Pancakes 34
    Smoked Salmon and Cream Cheese Bagels 35
    Veggie and Cheese Breakfast Frittata 35
    Breakfast Tacos 36
    Maple Bacon-Wrapped Sausages 37
    Peanut Butter and Banana Stuffed French Toast 38
    Mixed Berry Breakfast Cobbler 39

Chapter 6: Lunch Recipes 41

    Crispy Chicken Tenders 41
    Veggie-Stuffed Quesadillas 42
    Classic BLT Sandwich 43

Mediterranean Falafel Wrap 44
Zesty Buffalo Cauliflower Bites 45
Teriyaki Salmon Dish 46
Spinach and Feta Stuffed Mushrooms 47
BBQ Pulled Pork Sliders 48
Sweet Potato Fries 49
Caprese Panini 49
Southwest Quinoa Salad 50
Teriyaki Chicken Rice Dish 51
Crispy Eggplant Parmesan 52
Thai-Inspired Peanut Noodles 53
BBQ Grilled Cheese Sandwich 54
Lemon Garlic Shrimp Pasta 55
Veggie Packed Fried Rice 56
Hawaiian BBQ Chicken Pizza 58
Creamy Tomato Basil Soup 58
Spicy Buffalo Cauliflower Tacos 59
Vegetarian Stuffed Bell Peppers 60
Chicken Fajita Quesadillas 61

Chapter 7: Dinner Recipes 64

Crispy Air-Fried Chicken Tenders 64
Air-Fried Salmon with Lemon-Dill Sauce 65
Crispy Air-Fried Vegetable Spring Rolls 66
Air-Fried Honey BBQ Chicken Wings 67
Garlic Parmesan Air-Fried Potato Wedges 67
Crunchy Air-Fried Shrimp Tacos 68
Air-Fried Vegetable Stir-Fry 69
Air-Fried Beef and Broccoli 70
Air-Fried Stuffed Bell Peppers 71
Air-Fried Veggie Quesadillas 72
Air-Fried Teriyaki Chicken Skewers 73
Air-Fried Veggie and Quinoa Stuffed Peppers 74
Air-Fried Coconut Shrimp 75
Air-Fried Sausage and Pepper Hoagies 76
Air-Fried Sweet Potato Fries 77
Air-Fried BBQ Pulled Pork Sandwiches 77
Air-Fried Cajun Shrimp and Grits 78
Air-Fried Buffalo Cauliflower Bites 79
Air-Fried Lemon Herb Whole Chicken 80

Chapter 8: Dessert Recipes 82

    Cinnamon Sugar Donut Holes 82

    Chocolate Lava Cake 84

    Apple Crisp 85

    Blueberry Lemon Muffins 86

    Banana Fritters 87

    Strawberry Shortcake 88

    Raspberry Chocolate Turnovers 89

    Peach Cobbler 89

    Peanut Butter Chocolate Cookies 90

    Churros with Chocolate Sauce 91

    Chocolate-Dipped Strawberries 92

    Mini Apple Pies 93

    Pumpkin Spice Bites 94

    Lemon Bars 95

    Coconut Macaroons 96

    Rice Krispies Treats 97

    Chocolate Peanut Butter Banana Bites 98

    Mixed Berry Parfait 99

    Chia Pudding Parfait 99

Conclusion 101

Introduction

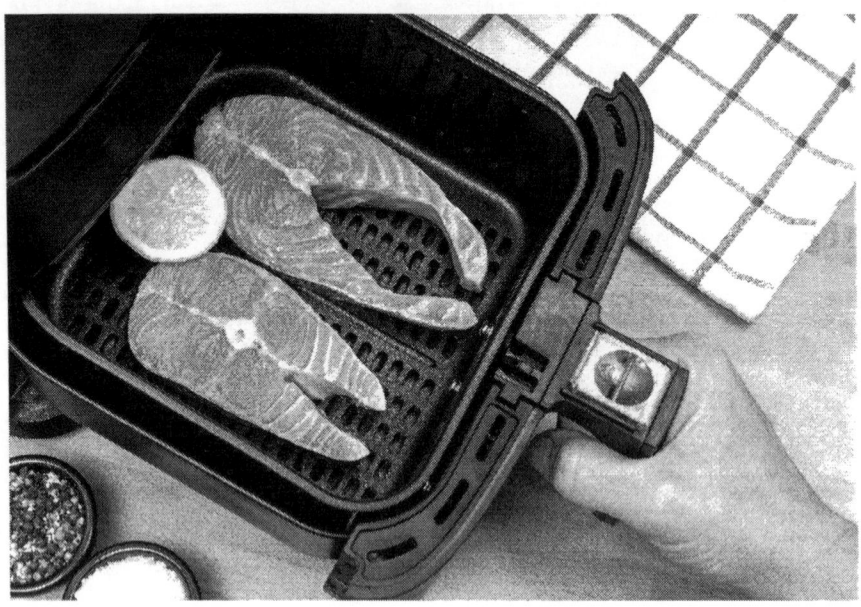

In a world where culinary innovation meets modern convenience, there emerges a kitchen warrior like no other – the Ninja Air Fryer. With its sleek design and the power to transform ordinary ingredients into extraordinary dishes, this kitchen marvel has taken the culinary world by storm. Are you ready to embark on a gastronomic adventure that's not just healthy but also incredibly delicious? Welcome to the realm of the Ninja Air Fryer Cookbook, where the art of air frying is elevated to new heights, and your taste buds are about to embark on a flavor-packed journey like never before. Whether you're a seasoned home chef or a novice in the kitchen, this cookbook is your ultimate guide to mastering the art of air frying with precision, creativity, and flair. Join us as we unlock the secrets of the Ninja Air Fryer and ignite your passion for cooking with a tantalizing array of recipes that will leave you craving more. Get ready to unleash the ninja within you and revolutionize the way you cook!

Ninja Air Fryer Cookbook for Beginners:

2000 Days of Crispy, Healthy, and Effortless Gourmet Delights | Transforming Everyday Ingredients into Culinary Masterpieces

By:
Asher Ellard

© **Copyright 2024 - All rights reserved.**

The contents of this book may not be reproduced, duplicated, or transmitted without the direct written permission of the author or publisher.

Under no circumstances will the publisher or author be held liable for any damages, recovery, or financial loss due to the information contained in this book. Neither directly nor indirectly.

Legal Notice:

This book is protected by copyright. This book is for personal use only. You may not modify, distribute, sell, use, quote, or paraphrase any part or content of this book without the permission of the author or publisher.

Disclaimer Notice:

Please note that the information contained in this document is for educational and entertainment purposes only. Every effort has been made to present accurate, current, reliable, and complete information. No warranties of any kind are stated or implied. The reader acknowledges that the author is not offering legal, financial, medical, or professional advice. The contents of this book have been taken from various sources. Please consult a licensed professional before attempting any of the techniques described in this book.

By reading this document, the reader agrees that under no circumstances will the author be liable for any direct or indirect loss arising from the use of the information contained in this document, including but not limited to - errors, omissions, or inaccuracies.

Chapter 1:
The history of The Ninja Air Fryer

The Ninja Air Fryer, a modern marvel in the world of kitchen appliances, represents the culmination of centuries of culinary evolution. To understand its significance, we must embark on a journey through time, exploring the historical milestones that led to the creation of this remarkable kitchen device.

Ancient Origins of Frying:

Frying food, the essence of the Ninja Air Fryer's technique, has ancient origins dating back to the earliest human civilizations. Millennia ago, our ancestors discovered the transformative power of hot oil to cook food to perfection. While the exact origin of frying remains elusive, evidence of deep-frying techniques can be traced back to ancient Mesopotamia, where cooks used a simple method of immersing food in boiling oil.

The Birth of Tempura:

Fast forward to 16th-century Japan, where the technique of deep frying received a unique twist. Portuguese Jesuit missionaries introduced the Japanese to tempura, a method of frying food in a light, airy batter. This culinary cross-pollination marked a pivotal moment in the evolution of frying techniques, as it combined the art of deep frying with a newfound appreciation for crispy textures.

The Emergence of Ninja Cuisine:

The term "Ninja" evokes images of stealthy warriors from feudal Japan, but the connection between ninjas and air frying is more symbolic than historical. However, it's worth noting that the ninja's legendary resourcefulness and adaptability align with the innovative spirit behind the Ninja Air Fryer. Just as ninjas mastered unconventional techniques, so too does this appliance revolutionize the way we cook.

The Age of Convection Ovens:

Before the Ninja Air Fryer, the concept of convection cooking was already well-established. Convection ovens, which circulated hot air to cook food evenly, had been in use for decades. However, they were often huge, expensive, and not readily accessible to the average home cook.

The Birth of the Air Fryer:

The true precursor to the Ninja Air Fryer can be traced back to the early 21st century when a small appliance known as the "hot air fryer" or "air fryer" began gaining popularity. The first air fryers utilized the principles of convection cooking to mimic the results of deep frying with significantly less oil. These early models were limited in capacity and functionality, but they sparked a culinary revolution by offering a healthier alternative to traditional frying methods.

Ninja's Entry into the Kitchen:

The Ninja brand, known for its innovation in kitchen appliances, recognized the potential of air frying and decided to take it to the next level. In 2003, Ninja introduced the Ninja Air Fryer to the market, setting a new standard for air frying technology. With its sleek design, user-friendly interface, and advanced cooking capabilities, it quickly gained a dedicated following among home cooks eager to enjoy their favorite fried foods without the guilt.

The Science Behind Air Frying:

At the heart of the Ninja Air Fryer's success lies the science of air frying. This culinary innovation relies on a powerful convection fan that circulates superheated air around the food, creating a crispy, golden exterior while maintaining moisture and flavor on the inside. By using only a fraction of the oil required for traditional frying, the Ninja Air Fryer allows users to enjoy the indulgence of fried food with fewer calories and less fat.

Evolution of the Ninja Air Fryer:

Since its introduction, the Ninja Air Fryer has gone through multiple iterations, each one more advanced than the last. These improvements have included increased cooking capacity, enhanced precision controls, and the integration of smart technology. The goal has always been to empower home cooks with the tools they need to create restaurant-quality dishes in the comfort of their own kitchens.

Ninja's Recipe Revolution:

One of the Ninja Air Fryer's most significant contributions to modern cuisine is its role in inspiring a new wave of recipes and culinary creativity. Home cooks around the world have embraced the versatility of this appliance, experimenting with a wide range of dishes from crispy chicken wings to sweet potato fries to decadent desserts. The Ninja Air Fryer has become a canvas for culinary innovation, sparking a resurgence of interest in home cooking.

The Impact on Health and Wellness:

Beyond its convenience and versatility, the Ninja Air Fryer has made a substantial impact on the health and wellness of its users. By reducing the need for excessive oil in cooking, it has helped individuals make healthier dietary choices. This shift towards a more health-conscious approach to cooking aligns with the growing awareness of the importance of balanced nutrition in today's society.

Cultural Influence and Global Adoption:

The Ninja Air Fryer's influence has transcended borders and culinary traditions. It has found its put in kitchens across the globe, from North America to Asia, and everywhere in between. Its ability to adapt to various cuisines and cooking styles has made it a beloved tool in both professional and amateur kitchens.

The Future of Air Frying:

As we look to the future, it's clear that the Ninja Air Fryer and similar appliances will continue to evolve. With advancements in technology and a growing focus on sustainability, we can expect to see even more innovative features, improved energy efficiency, and a broader range of culinary possibilities.

Chapter 2:
Ninja Air Fryer Techniques

In the ever-evolving landscape of culinary technology, the Ninja Air Fryer has emerged as a game-changer, offering home cooks an efficient and healthy way to prepare delicious meals. This versatile kitchen appliance harnesses the power of hot air circulation to create crispy, golden textures with a fraction of the oil traditionally required. But to truly become a Ninja in the realm of air fryer cooking, one must delve into the techniques and tips that make this appliance shine.

Understanding the Basics

Before we delve into the intricacies of Ninja Air Fryer cooking, let's start with the fundamentals:

1. **Preheating:** Just like an oven, it's essential to Set the temperature of your Ninja Air Fryer. This ensures that your food begins cooking immediately when you put it inside, leading to a crispy exterior.
2. **Temperature Control:** Ninja Air Fryers typically have adjustable temperature settings, usually ranging from 180°F to 400°F (82°C to 204°C). Different recipes will require various temperature settings, so understanding this is crucial.

3. **Timing Matters:** Accurate timing is crucial in air frying. Most recipes will provide suggested Cooking Period: s, but be prepared to adjust based on your specific appliance and the quantity of food you're cooking.
4. **Shaking and Flipping:** To ensure even cooking, shake or flip your food halfway through the cooking process. This helps in achieving uniform crispiness.
5. **Oil or Spray:** While air frying is inherently low in oil, a light spritz of cooking spray or a drizzle of oil can enhance the texture and flavor of your dishes.

Techniques for Perfect Results

Now, let's explore the advanced techniques that elevate your Ninja Air Fryer cooking game:

1. Layering and Stacking:

- To maximize your air fryer's capacity, you can layer or stack certain foods. However, ensure there's enough space for air circulation. Use accessories like racks or skewers to create multiple levels of cooking.

2. Breading and Coating:

- Achieve a crispy and golden exterior by breading or coating your ingredients. Dip them in beaten eggs, coat with breadcrumbs or flour, and then air fry. This technique works wonders for chicken tenders, onion rings, and more.

3. Marinating and Seasoning:

- Marinating your proteins or vegetables before air frying can infuse them with flavor. Use your favorite marinades, spices, and herbs to enhance the taste of your dishes.

4. Par-Cooking:

- For foods with varying Cooking Period: s, consider par-cooking. Start with ingredients that need longer air frying, then add the quicker-cooking items halfway through.

5. Temperature Probing:

- Invest in a kitchen thermometer to ensure your meats are cooked to perfection. Different proteins have distinct ideal internal temperatures for safe consumption.

6. Dehydration:

- Ninja Air Fryers often come with a dehydration function. Use this to make healthy snacks like fruit chips or vegetable crisps by removing moisture from your ingredients.

7. Roasting and Baking:

- Exploit the versatility of your Ninja Air Fryer by roasting vegetables or baking small cakes, muffins, or even cookies. Experiment with different cookware and molds that fit inside the appliance.

8. Custom Accessories:

- Ninja offers various accessories like grill grates, skewer stands, and multi-layer racks. These expand your air frying capabilities, allowing you to grill, skewer, or create layered dishes effortlessly.

Tips for Success

Now that you're familiar with the techniques, here are some tips to ensure your Ninja Air Fryer cooking ventures are consistently successful:

1. **Keep it Dry:** Excess moisture can hinder crisping. Pat ingredients dry before placing them in the air fryer.
2. **Don't Overcrowd:** Leave enough space between food items for proper air circulation. Overcrowding can result in uneven cooking.
3. **Use Parchment Paper:** To prevent sticking and make cleanup easier, use parchment paper or silicone mats for certain recipes.
4. **Monitor Progress:** Keep an eye on your cooking, especially the first time you try a new recipe. Adjust timing or temperature as needed.
5. **Prevent Smoke:** Some recipes may release fats or oils that can produce smoke. To avoid this, empty the drip tray as necessary and use a higher temperature setting if needed.

6. **Experiment and Adapt:** Don't be afraid to experiment with your Ninja Air Fryer. Adapt recipes to your taste and take notes for future reference.
7. **Maintenance:** Regularly clean the air fryer's components, including the rack, rack, and drip tray, to ensure consistent performance and longevity.

Chapter 3:
Ninja Air Fryer Cooking Advantages

In this exploration of the Ninja Air Fryer, we'll delve into the myriad advantages it brings to your culinary adventures, showcasing how it revolutionizes the way we cook and eat.

1. Healthier Eating, Effortlessly

At the heart of the Ninja Air Fryer's appeal lies its ability to transform our eating habits for the better. By using hot air circulation to cook food, it offers a healthier alternative to traditional frying methods. Gone are the days of submerging ingredients in copious amounts of oil; the Ninja Air Fryer requires only a fraction of the oil to achieve that crispy, golden texture we all love. This means you can enjoy your favorite fried foods with significantly reduced fat content, making it an excellent choice for those looking to maintain a healthier diet without sacrificing flavor.

2. Precision Cooking

One of the standout advantages of the Ninja Air Fryer is its precision. Equipped with advanced temperature control and Cooking Period: settings, it ensures that your dishes are cooked to perfection every time. Whether you're preparing delicate pastries, succulent meats, or crispy fries, you can fine-tune the settings to achieve the desired level of doneness. This precision cooking eliminates the guesswork and potential for overcooking or undercooking, allowing you to consistently create restaurant-quality meals in the comfort of your own kitchen.

3. Versatility Redefined

The Ninja Air Fryer is not limited to just frying. It's a versatile kitchen companion that can roast, bake, grill, and even dehydrate. This versatility opens up a world of culinary possibilities, from juicy rotisserie chicken to crispy vegetable chips. With the right recipe and a touch of creativity, you can use this appliance to prepare a wide range of dishes that cater to diverse tastes and dietary preferences. It's like having a miniature kitchen arsenal at your disposal.

4. Speedy Cooking

In our fast-paced lives, time is often a precious commodity. The Ninja Air Fryer respects your time by significantly reducing cooking durations. It's remarkably efficient, with its rapid hot air circulation ensuring that food cooks evenly and quickly. No more waiting for the oven to preheat or frying pans to heat up; the Ninja Air Fryer heats up in a matter of seconds, allowing you to get meals on the table in record time. This makes it an excellent tool for busy families and individuals looking to prepare delicious, wholesome meals without the hassle.

5. Easy Cleanup

Cooking can be a joy, but cleaning up afterward can often be a dreaded chore. Fortunately, the Ninja Air Fryer minimizes the mess. Its non-stick cooking rack and tray are designed for easy cleaning, either by hand or in the dishwasher. Say goodbye to scrubbing oil-soaked pans or dealing with stubborn food residue. With the Ninja Air Fryer, you can savor the flavors of your creations without the worry of an arduous cleanup process.

6. Energy Efficiency

In an era where sustainability is at the forefront of our minds, the Ninja Air Fryer stands out as an energy-efficient appliance. Compared to traditional ovens, it consumes significantly less energy, making it an eco-friendly choice. This not only reduces your carbon footprint but also translates to cost savings on your energy bills over time. It's a win-win for both your wallet and the environment.

7. Family-Friendly Cooking

The Ninja Air Fryer is a family-friendly appliance that encourages shared cooking experiences. Its simplicity and safety features make it accessible to children and teens who want to get involved in the kitchen. By involving the whole family in meal preparation, you can create lasting memories and instill healthy eating habits from an early age.

8. Flavor Enhancement

Contrary to popular belief, healthy eating doesn't mean sacrificing flavor. In fact, the Ninja Air Fryer enhances the natural flavors of ingredients. The hot air circulation seals in juices, resulting in dishes that are moist on the inside and delightfully crispy on the outside. This means you can enjoy guilt-free indulgence with every bite, as the flavors are intensified, not compromised.

9. Reduced Odors

Cooking certain dishes can often fill your kitchen with lingering, less-than-pleasant odors. With the Ninja Air Fryer, this is no longer a concern. Its enclosed cooking chamber and effective ventilation system keep odors to a minimum. Say goodbye to the lingering smell of frying oil or overcooked fish, and hello to a kitchen that remains fresh and inviting.

10. Culinary Creativity Unleashed

Last but certainly not least, the Ninja Air Fryer encourages culinary creativity. Its versatility and precision allow you to experiment with a wide range of recipes and cuisines. From experimenting with exotic spices to reinventing classic comfort foods, this appliance empowers you to become a kitchen innovator. You'll find yourself trying out new dishes, flavors, and techniques that you may have never considered before.

Chapter 4:
Ninja Air Fryer Maintenance

1. **General Maintenance Steps**

1. Unplug and Cool Down

Before performing any maintenance on your Ninja Air Fryer, always unplug it and allow it to cool down completely. Safety should be your top priority, so never attempt to clean or maintain a hot appliance.

2. Disassemble the Parts

The Ninja Air Fryer typically consists of several removable parts, including the frying rack, crisper plate, and drip pan. Carefully remove these components for thorough cleaning. Refer to your user manual for specific instructions on disassembly.

3. Wash Removable Parts

Most of the removable parts of your Ninja Air Fryer are dishwasher safe, making cleanup a breeze. However, it's advisable to wash them by hand using warm, soapy water. This ensures that any stubborn residues are removed effectively. Use a soft sponge or cloth to avoid scratching the non-stick surfaces.

4. Clean the Interior

To clean the interior of the air fryer, use a damp cloth or sponge to wipe away any food particles or oil. Avoid using abrasive materials or harsh chemicals, as they can damage the appliance's interior.

5. Check the Heating Element

Inspect the heating element for any buildup of food debris or oil. If you notice any residue, gently wipe it away with a damp cloth. Ensure the heating element is completely dry before reassembling the appliance.

6. Clean the Exterior

Wipe down the exterior of the Ninja Air Fryer with a damp cloth to remove any splatters or spills. Pay special attention to the control panel, making sure no liquids or crumbs have entered the buttons or display.

2. Deep Cleaning and Maintenance

In addition to the routine steps mentioned above, it's essential to perform deep cleaning and maintenance periodically to address more stubborn residues and ensure optimal performance.

1. Deodorize with Vinegar

To eliminate any lingering odors from previous cooking sessions, put a dish of white vinegar in the air fryer rack and run the appliance at a low temperature for a few Min. This will help neutralize odors and leave your air fryer smelling fresh.

2. Scrub the Rack and Pan

For stubborn, baked-on residues on the frying rack and crisper plate, soak them in warm, soapy water for a few hrs. Then, use a non-abrasive sponge or brush to scrub away any remaining debris. Rinse thoroughly and allow them to air dry.

3. Clean the Exterior Thoroughly

Wipe the exterior of the Ninja Air Fryer with a mixture of warm water and mild detergent. Use a soft cloth or sponge to remove any oil or stains. Ensure that you dry the exterior thoroughly to prevent any damage to the appliance.

4. Check the Ventilation

The air fryer's ventilation system can accumulate dust and debris over time, potentially affecting its performance. Use a soft brush or a can of compressed air to clean the vents carefully. Be gentle to avoid pushing debris further into the appliance.

5. Lubricate Moving Parts

Some Ninja Air Fryer models have moving parts, such as the rotating paddle in a multi-function air fryer. Periodically, apply a food-safe lubricant to ensure smooth operation. Refer to your user manual for specific instructions on lubrication.

3. Troubleshooting and Maintenance Tips

1. Addressing Sticky Residues

If you encounter stubborn, sticky residues on the interior surfaces, try using a mixture of baking soda and water to create a paste. Apply the paste to the affected areas, let it sit for a few Min, and then scrub gently with a non-abrasive sponge or cloth.

2. Dealing with Stains

For stains on the exterior of the air fryer, you can make a paste using equal parts baking soda and water. Apply the paste to the stains, let it sit for a few Min, and then wipe it away with a damp cloth.

3. Regularly Check the Power Cord

Inspect the power cord for any signs of wear or damage. If you notice any exposed wires or fraying, it's crucial to reput the cord immediately to avoid safety hazards.

4. Keep the Air Intake and Exhaust Clear

Ensure that the air intake and exhaust openings are always free from obstructions. Dust and debris can accumulate around these areas, affecting the air fryer's performance.

5. Store Properly

When not in use, store your Ninja Air Fryer in a cool, dry put. Make sure it is covered or protected from dust and potential damage. Avoid stacking heavy objects on top of the appliance.

4. Safety Considerations

Maintaining your Ninja Air Fryer is not only about keeping it clean and functional but also about ensuring safety in the kitchen.

1. Regular Inspections

Periodically inspect your air fryer for any signs of wear, damage, or malfunction. If you notice any issues, contact Ninja customer support or a qualified technician for repairs.

2. Use Proper Utensils

Always use utensils that are safe for non-stick surfaces when cooking in your air fryer. Metal utensils can scratch and damage the non-stick coating.

3. Avoid Overfilling

To ensure even cooking and proper air circulation, avoid overfilling the frying rack. Follow the manufacturer's guidelines for maximum fill levels.

4. Stay Alert

Never leave your Ninja Air Fryer unattended while it's in operation. Accidents can happen quickly, so always keep an eye on your air fryer.

Chapter 5: Breakfast Recipes

1. Crispy Breakfast Potatoes

- Preparation Period: 10 Min
- Cooking Period: 20 Min
- Serves:4

Ingredients needed:

- 4 medium russet potatoes, washed and diced
- 10g of olive oil
- 5 g of paprika
- 3 g of garlic powder
- Sea salt and pepper as desired
- Fresh parsley, diced (for garnish)

Preparation Process

1. Set the temperature of your Ninja Air Fryer to 400°F (200°C).

2. In a huge dish , toss the diced potatoes with olive oil, paprika, garlic powder, Sea salt , and pepper until evenly coated.
3. Put the seasoned potatoes in the air fryer rack in a single layer.
4. Cook for 15-20 Min, shaking the rack every 5 Min, until the potatoes are cripsy and crispy.
5. Sprinkle with fresh parsley before serving.

Serving Total:

- Kcal:180 kcal
- Carbs: 29g
- Fat: 7g
- Protein: 3g

2. Fluffy Blueberry Pancakes

- Preparation Period: 10 Min
- Cooking Period: 6 Min
- Serves:2

Ingredients needed:

- 200g of wheat flour
- 5 g of sugar
- 5 g of leavening
- 3 g of baking soda
- 2 g of Sea salt
- 200g of buttermilk
- 1 huge egg
- 10g of unSea salt ed butter, softened
- 50g of fresh blueberries

Preparation Process

1. In a mixing dish, whisk together the flour, sugar, leavening , baking soda, and Sea salt .
2. In a separate dish , whisk together the buttermilk, egg, and softened butter.

3. Pour the wet ingredients into the dry ingredients and stir until just combined. Be careful not to overmix; some lumps are okay.
4. Gently fold in the blueberries.
5. Set the temperature of your Ninja Air Fryer to 350°F (180°C).
6. Oil the air fryer rack with a little butter or oil.
7. Drop spoonfuls of pancake batter onto the rack, leaving space between each pancake.
8. Cook for 3 Min, flip the pancakes, and cook for another 3 Min or until they're cripsy.
9. Serve with maple syrup or your favorite toppings.

Serving Total:

- Kcal:350 kcal
- Carbs: 52g
- Fat: 11g
- Protein: 9g

3. Veggie Breakfast Burritos

- Preparation Period: 15 Min
- Cooking Period: 10 Min
- Serves:4

Ingredients needed:

- 4 huge eggs, beaten
- 50g of diced bell peppers
- 50g of diced onions
- 50g of diced tomatoes
- 50g of diced cheddar cheese
- Sea salt and pepper as desired
- 4 huge flour tortillas

Preparation Process

1. Set the temperature of your Ninja Air Fryer to 350°F (180°C).

2. In a non-stick frypan, sauté the bell peppers, onions, and tomatoes until softened, about 3-4 Min.
3. Pour the beaten eggs over the sautéed vegetables and scramble until fully cooked.
4. Lay out a flour tortilla and spoon some of the scrambled eggs onto the center.
5. Sprinkle with diced cheddar cheese and season with Sea salt and pepper.
6. Fold in the sides of the tortilla and roll it up, creating a burrito.
7. Put the burrito seam-side down in the air fryer rack.
8. Repeat with the remaining tortillas.
9. Air fry for 5-7 Min until the burritos are crispy and lightly browned.
10. Serve with salsa or hot sauce if desired.

Serving Total:

- Kcal:220 kcal
- Carbs: 19g
- Fat: 11g
- Protein: 11g

4. Banana-Nut Oatmeal Muffins

- Preparation Period: 15 Min
- Cooking Period: 15 Min
- Serves:6

Ingredients needed:

- 200g of rolled oats
- 200g of mashed ripe bananas (about 2 bananas)
- 50g of plain Greek yogurt
- 50g of honey
- 1 huge egg
- 5 g of vanilla essence
- 3 g of crushed cinnamon
- 3 g of baking soda
- 3 g of leavening
- 2 g of Sea salt
- 50g of diced nuts (walnuts or pecans)

Preparation Process

1. In a dish , combine the rolled oats, mashed bananas, Greek yogurt, honey, egg, vanilla essence, crushed cinnamon, baking soda, leavening , and Sea salt . Mix until well combined.
2. Fold in the diced nuts.
3. Set the temperature of your Ninja Air Fryer to 325°F (160°C).
4. Line muffin cups with paper liners.
5. Divide the muffin batter evenly among the muffin cups.
6. Put the muffin cups in the air fryer rack in batches if necessary.
7. Air fry for 12-15 Min until the muffins are firm to the touch and lightly browned.
8. Allow the muffins to cool before serving.

Serving Total:

- Kcal:240 kcal
- Carbs: 38g
- Fat: 8g
- Protein: 6g

5. Spinach and Feta Breakfast Quesadillas

- Preparation Period: 10 Min
- Cooking Period: 6 Min
- Serves:2

Ingredients needed:

- 2 huge flour tortillas
- 4 huge eggs, beaten
- 200g of baby spinach, diced
- 50g of crumbled feta cheese
- Sea salt and pepper as desired
- Cooking spray or oil for greasing

Preparation Process

1. Set the temperature of your Ninja Air Fryer to 350°F (180°C).

2. In a non-stick frypan, scramble the eggs until they are almost fully cooked but slightly runny.
3. Put one flour tortilla on a clean surface.
4. Sprinkle half of the diced spinach evenly on one half of the tortilla.
5. Spoon half of the scrambled eggs over the spinach.
6. Sprinkle half of the crumbled feta cheese on top.
7. Fold the other half of the tortilla over to create a half-moon shape.
8. Lightly oil the air fryer rack with cooking spray or oil.
9. Put the quesadilla in the rack and air fry for 3 Min per side, or until it's crispy and the cheese is softened .
10. Repeat the process for the second quesadilla.
11. Let them cool for a minute before slicing into wedges.

Serving Total:

- Kcal:380 kcal
- Carbs: 26g
- Fat: 22g
- Protein: 19g

6. Greek Yogurt Parfait

- Preparation Period: 5 Min
- Cooking Period: 0 Min
- Serves:2

Ingredients needed:

- 200g of Greek yogurt
- 50g of granola
- 50g of mixed berries (strawberries, blueberries, raspberries)
- 10g of honey
- 2 g of vanilla essence
- Fresh mint leaves for garnish

Preparation Process

1. In a dish , mix the Greek yogurt, honey, and vanilla essence until well combined.

2. In serving glasses or dish s, layer the yogurt mixture, granola, and mixed berries.
3. Repeat the layers as desired.
4. Garnish with fresh mint leaves.
5. Serve immediately as a refreshing and healthy breakfast option.

Serving Total:

- Kcal:270 kcal
- Carbs: 41g
- Fat: 5g
- Protein: 17g

7. Avocado Toast with Poached Eggs

- Preparation Period: 10 Min
- Cooking Period: 5 Min
- Serves:2

Ingredients needed:

- 2 slices of whole-grain bread
- 1 ripe avocado, diced
- 2 huge eggs
- Sea salt and pepper as desired
- Red pepper flakes (optional)
- Fresh cilantro leaves for garnish

Preparation Process

1. Toast the slices of whole-grain bread in your Ninja Air Fryer until they are crisp and cripsy.
2. While the bread is toasting, fill a shallow pan with water and bring it to a gentle simmer.
3. Crack one egg into a small dish .
4. Create a gentle whirlpool in the simmering water using a spoon, then gently slide the egg into the whirlpool.
5. Poach the egg for 3-4 Min until the white is set, but the yolk is still runny.
6. Remove the poached egg with a slotted spoon and drain any excess water.

7. Repeat the poaching process with the second egg.
8. Spread the diced avocado evenly over the toasted bread slices.
9. Put a poached egg on top of each slice.
10. Season with Sea salt , pepper, and red pepper flakes if desired.
11. Garnish with fresh cilantro leaves before serving.

Serving Total:

- Kcal:250 kcal
- Carbs: 22g
- Fat: 15g
- Protein: 9g

8. Cinnamon Sugar French Toast Sticks

- Preparation Period: 10 Min
- Cooking Period: 8 Min
- Serves:4

Ingredients needed:

- 4 slices of thick-cut bread
- 2 huge eggs
- 50g of milk
- 50g of processed sugar
- 5 g of crushed cinnamon
- 3 g of vanilla essence
- Butter or cooking spray for greasing

Preparation Process

1. Cut each slice of bread into sticks.
2. In a shallow dish , whisk together the eggs, milk, processed sugar , crushed cinnamon, and vanilla essence.
3. Set the temperature of your Ninja Air Fryer to 350°F (180°C).
4. Oil the air fryer rack with butter or cooking spray.
5. Dip each bread stick into the egg mixture, making sure it's coated evenly, and put it in the air fryer rack.

6. Cook for 4 Min, flip the sticks, and cook for another 4 Min until they are cripsy and crispy.
7. Serve with maple syrup for dipping.

Serving Total:

- Kcal:220 kcal
- Carbs: 33g
- Fat: 7g
- Protein: 7g

9. Breakfast Burrito Dish

- Preparation Period: 15 Min
- Cooking Period: 10 Min
- Serves:2

Ingredients needed:

- 200g of cooked quinoa
- 2 huge eggs
- 50g of black beans, drained and rinsed
- 50g of diced tomatoes
- 50g of diced red onions
- 50g of diced bell peppers
- 50g of diced cheddar cheese
- Sea salt and pepper as desired
- Fresh cilantro leaves for garnish
- Salsa for topping (optional)

Preparation Process

1. Set the temperature of your Ninja Air Fryer to 350°F (180°C).
2. In a frypan, sauté the diced red onions and bell peppers until softened, about 3-4 Min.
3. Add the black beans and diced tomatoes to the frypan and cook for an additional 2 Min.

4. In a separate non-stick frypan, scramble the eggs until they are cooked to your preference.
5. In serving dish s, layer the cooked quinoa, sautéed vegetables, scrambled eggs, and diced cheddar cheese.
6. Season with Sea salt and pepper.
7. Garnish with fresh cilantro leaves and salsa if desired.

Serving Total:

- Kcal:350 kcal
- Carbs: 35g
- Fat: 16g
- Protein: 17g

10. Healthy Fruit Smoothie

- Preparation Period: 5 Min
- Cooking Period: 0 Min
- Serves:2

Ingredients needed:

- 1 ripe banana
- 200g of mixed frozen berries (strawberries, blueberries, raspberries)
- 200g of spinach leaves
- 200g of sugarless almond milk
- 5 g of honey (optional)
- Ice cubes (optional)

Preparation Process

1. Put all the ingredients into a blender.
2. Blend until smooth and creamy.
3. Add ice cubes if you prefer a colder smoothie.
4. Taste and add honey if you desire extra sweetness.
5. Pour into glasses and serve immediately as a refreshing and nutritious breakfast.

Serving Total:

- Kcal:150 kcal
- Carbs: 37g
- Fat: 1g
- Protein: 2g

11. Breakfast Stuffed Bell Peppers

- Preparation Period: 15 Min
- Cooking Period: 20 Min
- Serves:2

Ingredients needed:

- 2 huge bell peppers (red, yellow, or green)
- 4 huge eggs
- 50g of cooked sausage or bacon, crumbled (optional)
- 50g of diced tomatoes
- 50g of diced onions
- 50g of diced cheddar cheese
- Sea salt and pepper as desired
- Fresh parsley for garnish

Preparation Process

1. Cut the tops off the bell peppers and remove the seeds and membranes.
2. In a dish, combine the crumbled sausage or bacon (if using), diced tomatoes, diced onions, and diced cheddar cheese.
3. Carefully stuff the bell peppers with this mixture.
4. Set the temperature of your Ninja Air Fryer to 350°F (180°C).
5. Oil the air fryer rack with a little oil.
6. Put the stuffed bell peppers in the rack.
7. Crack an egg into each bell pepper.
8. Season with Sea salt and pepper.
9. Air fry for 15-20 Min until the egg whites are set, and the yolks are still slightly runny.
10. Garnish with fresh parsley before serving.

Serving Total:

- Kcal:280 kcal
- Carbs: 15g
- Fat: 18g
- Protein: 15g

12. Apple Cinnamon Breakfast Quinoa

- Preparation Period: 10 Min
- Cooking Period: 10 Min
- Serves:2

Ingredients needed:

- 200g of cooked quinoa
- 1 apple, diced
- 50g of diced nuts (walnuts or almonds)
- 50g of raisins or dried cranberries
- 5 g of honey
- 3 g of crushed cinnamon
- 2 g of vanilla essence
- Greek yogurt for topping (optional)

Preparation Process

1. In a dish, combine the cooked quinoa, diced apple, diced nuts, raisins or dried cranberries, honey, crushed cinnamon, and vanilla essence.
2. Mix until all ingredients are well incorporated.
3. Set the temperature of your Ninja Air Fryer to 350°F (180°C).
4. Transfer the quinoa mixture to an oven-safe dish or ramekin.
5. Air fry for 10 Min until it's heated through and the flavors meld together.
6. Serve with a dollop of Greek yogurt if desired.

Serving Total:

- Kcal:280 kcal
- Carbs: 46g
- Fat: 9g

- Protein: 6g

13. Sausage and Egg Breakfast Burritos

- Preparation Period: 15 Min
- Cooking Period: 6 Min
- Serves: 2

Ingredients needed:

- 4 huge eggs, beaten
- 2 sausage links, cooked and diced
- 50g of diced cheddar cheese
- 2 huge flour tortillas
- Sea salt and pepper as desired
- Cooking spray or oil for greasing

Preparation Process

1. Set the temperature of your Ninja Air Fryer to 350°F (180°C).
2. In a non-stick frypan, scramble the beaten eggs until they are cooked to your liking.
3. Put a flour tortilla on a clean surface.
4. Spread half of the scrambled eggs evenly on one half of the tortilla.
5. Add diced sausage and diced cheddar cheese on top.
6. Fold the other half of the tortilla over to create a half-moon shape.
7. Lightly oil the air fryer rack with cooking spray or oil.
8. Put the burrito in the rack, seam-side down.
9. Air fry for 3 Min per side, or until it's crispy and the cheese is softened.
10. Repeat the process for the second burrito.

Serving Total:

- Kcal: 480 kcal
- Carbs: 25g
- Fat: 35g
- Protein: 20g

14. Chocolate Banana Protein Pancakes

- Preparation Period: 15 Min
- Cooking Period: 6 Min
- Serves: 2

Ingredients needed:

- 1 ripe banana
- 2 huge eggs
- 50g of sugarless cocoa powder
- 50g of protein powder (chocolate or vanilla)
- 3 g of leavening
- 3 g of vanilla essence
- Cooking spray or oil for greasing

Preparation Process

1. In a blender, combine the ripe banana, eggs, cocoa powder, protein powder, leavening, and vanilla essence.
2. Blend until the batter is smooth.
3. Set the temperature of your Ninja Air Fryer to 350°F (180°C).
4. Oil the air fryer rack with cooking spray or oil.
5. Pour the pancake batter onto the rack to create small pancakes.
6. Air fry for 3 Min per side, or until they are cooked through.
7. Serve with a drizzle of honey or a dollop of Greek yogurt.

Serving Total:

- Kcal: 220 kcal
- Carbs: 28g
- Fat: 8g
- Protein: 15g

15. Smoked Salmon and Cream Cheese Bagels

- Preparation Period: 10 Min
- Cooking Period: 0 Min
- Serves: 2

Ingredients needed:

- 2 whole-grain bagels, diced and toasted
- 20g of cream cheese
- 4 slices of smoked salmon
- Red onion slices
- Capers (optional)
- Fresh dill for garnish

Preparation Process

1. Spread cream cheese on each toasted bagel half.
2. Layer with smoked salmon, red onion slices, and capers if desired.
3. Garnish with fresh dill.
4. Serve as an elegant and satisfying breakfast.

Serving Total:

- Kcal: 340 kcal
- Carbs: 40g
- Fat: 10g
- Protein: 20g

16. Veggie and Cheese Breakfast Frittata

- Preparation Period: 15 Min
- Cooking Period: 15 Min
- Serves: 4

Ingredients needed:

- 6 huge eggs
- 50g of diced bell peppers (a mix of colors)

- 50g of diced onions
- 50g of diced tomatoes
- 50g of diced cheddar cheese
- Sea salt and pepper as desired
- Fresh chives for garnish

Preparation Process

1. Set the temperature of your Ninja Air Fryer to 350°F (180°C).
2. In a dish, whisk together the eggs, diced bell peppers, diced onions, diced tomatoes, diced cheddar cheese, Sea salt, and pepper.
3. Pour the egg mixture into an oiled oven-safe dish or pan that fits in the air fryer.
4. Air fry for 15 Min or until the frittata is set in the center and the edges are cripsy.
5. Garnish with fresh chives before serving.
6. Slice and enjoy your wholesome breakfast frittata.

Serving Total:

- Kcal:220 kcal
- Carbs: 6g
- Fat: 15g
- Protein: 14g

17. Breakfast Tacos

- Preparation Period: 10 Min
- Cooking Period: 6 Min
- Serves:2

Ingredients needed:

- 4 small corn or flour tortillas
- 4 huge eggs
- 50g of cooked and crumbled breakfast sausage
- 50g of diced bell peppers
- 50g of diced onions
- 50g of diced Monterey Jack cheese
- Salsa and diced cilantro for topping (optional)

- Cooking spray or oil for greasing

Preparation Process

1. Set the temperature of your Ninja Air Fryer to 350°F (180°C).
2. In a non-stick frypan, scramble the eggs until they are cooked to your liking.
3. In another frypan, sauté the diced bell peppers and onions until softened.
4. Oil the air fryer rack with cooking spray or oil.
5. Put the tortillas in the rack and air fry for 2-3 Min until they are warm and slightly crispy.
6. Assemble the breakfast tacos by placing a portion of scrambled eggs, sautéed vegetables, crumbled breakfast sausage, and diced Monterey Jack cheese on each tortilla.
7. Top with salsa and diced cilantro if desired.

Serving Total:

- Kcal:370 kcal
- Carbs: 24g
- Fat: 21g
- Protein: 19g

18. Maple Bacon-Wrapped Sausages

- Preparation Period: 10 Min
- Cooking Period: 15 Min
- Serves:4

Ingredients needed:

- 8 cocktail sausages
- 4 slices of bacon, cut in half
- 10g of maple syrup
- Toothpicks for securing

Preparation Process

1. Set the temperature of your Ninja Air Fryer to 350°F (180°C).
2. Wrap each cocktail sausage with a half-slice of bacon and secure with a toothpick.

3. Put the wrapped sausages in the air fryer rack.
4. Air fry for 10 Min, turning the sausages halfway through the Cooking Period: .
5. Brush each sausage with maple syrup and continue to air fry for an additional 5 Min or until the bacon is crispy and caramelized.
6. Serve these sweet and savory delights as a tasty breakfast treat.

Serving Total:

- Kcal:240 kcal
- Carbs: 6g
- Fat: 19g
- Protein: 10g

19. Peanut Butter and Banana Stuffed French Toast

- Preparation Period: 15 Min
- Cooking Period: 8 Min
- Serves:2

Ingredients needed:

- 4 slices of thick-cut bread
- 10g of peanut butter
- 1 banana, diced
- 2 huge eggs
- 50g of milk
- 3 g of crushed cinnamon
- 3 g of vanilla essence
- Cooking spray or oil for greasing

Preparation Process

1. Set the temperature of your Ninja Air Fryer to 350°F (180°C).
2. Spread peanut butter on two slices of bread.
3. Top with banana slices and cover with the remaining bread slices to make sandwiches.
4. In a shallow dish, whisk together the eggs, milk, crushed cinnamon, and vanilla essence.

5. Dip each sandwich into the egg mixture, making sure it's coated evenly.
6. Oil the air fryer rack with cooking spray or oil.
7. Put the stuffed French toast sandwiches in the rack.
8. Air fry for 4 Min per side, or until they are cripsy and crispy.
9. Serve with a drizzle of maple syrup or a sprinkle of refined sugar .

Serving Total:

- Kcal:360 kcal
- Carbs: 41g
- Fat: 16g
- Protein: 13g

20. Mixed Berry Breakfast Cobbler

- Preparation Period: 15 Min
- Cooking Period: 20 Min
- Serves:4

Ingredients needed:

- 2 cups mixed berries (strawberries, blueberries, raspberries)
- 50g of processed sugar
- 3 g of lemon juice
- 200g of rolled oats
- 50g of wheat flour
- 50g of brown sugar
- 50g of unSea salt ed butter, softened
- 2 g of crushed cinnamon
- Vanilla ice cream for topping (optional)

Preparation Process

1. In a dish , combine the mixed berries, processed sugar , and lemon juice.
2. Set the temperature of your Ninja Air Fryer to 350°F (180°C).
3. Oil an oven-safe dish that fits in the air fryer.
4. Pour the berry mixture into the dish.

5. In another dish , mix the rolled oats, wheat flour , brown sugar, softened unSea salt ed butter, and crushed cinnamon until it forms a crumbly topping.
6. Sprinkle the oat topping evenly over the berries.
7. Air fry for 15-20 Min until the berry filling is bubbly, and the topping is cripsy.
8. Let it cool slightly before serving.
9. Top with vanilla ice cream for an indulgent breakfast treat.

Serving Total:

- Kcal:280 kcal
- Carbs: 48g
- Fat: 9g
- Protein: 4g

Chapter 6: Lunch Recipes

21. Crispy Chicken Tenders

- Preparation Period: 15 Min
- Cooking Period: 15 Min
- Serves: 4

Ingredients needed:

- 1 pound (450g) chicken tenders
- 200g of (240ml) buttermilk
- 200g of (120g) breadcrumbs
- 50g of (60g) crushed Parmesan cheese
- 5 g of paprika
- 3 g of garlic powder
- Sea salt and pepper as desired
- Cooking spray

Preparation Process

1. In a dish , combine the buttermilk, paprika, garlic powder, Sea salt , and pepper. Add the chicken tenders, ensuring they are fully coated. Marinate for 10 Min.
2. In a separate dish , mix breadcrumbs and crushed Parmesan cheese.
3. Dredge the marinated chicken tenders in the breadcrumb mixture, pressing firmly to adhere.
4. Set the temperature of your Ninja Air Fryer to 375°F (190°C).
5. Lightly oil the air fryer rack with cooking spray.
6. Put the breaded chicken tenders in one layer in the air fryer rack, ensuring they do not touch.
7. Air fry for 10-12 Min, turning halfway through, until the chicken tenders are cripsy and cooked through.
8. Serve with your favorite dipping sauce.

Serving Total

- Kcal:320 kcal
- Carbs: 18g
- Fat: 12g
- Protein: 32g

22. Veggie-Stuffed Quesadillas

- Preparation Period: 10 Min
- Cooking Period: 8 Min
- Serves:4

Ingredients needed:

- 4 huge whole-wheat tortillas
- 200g of (150g) diced cheddar cheese
- 1 bell pepper, finely diced
- 1 red onion, finely diced
- 200g of (150g) diced mushrooms
- 200g of (100g) baby spinach
- 5 g of olive oil
- Sea salt and pepper as desired

- Cooking spray

Preparation Process

1. Olive oil is heated in a frypan at a medium temperature. Bell pepper, red onion, and mushrooms should all be sautéed until tender. Once added, sauté the baby spinach until wilted. Use sea salt and pepper to season.
2. Lay out a tortilla and sprinkle with diced cheddar cheese.
3. Spoon the sautéed vegetable mixture evenly over the cheese.
4. Top with another tortilla and press gently to seal.
5. Set the temperature of your Ninja Air Fryer to 375°F (190°C).
6. Lightly oil the air fryer rack with cooking spray.
7. Carefully put the quesadilla in the air fryer and cook for 4 Min on each side until crispy and golden.
8. Remove, let it cool for a minute, then slice into wedges and serve.

Serving Total

- Kcal:290 kcal
- Carbs: 32g
- Fat: 14g
- Protein: 12g

23. Classic BLT Sandwich

- Preparation Period: 10 Min
- Cooking Period: 5 Min
- Serves:2

Ingredients needed:

- 4 slices of bread
- 8 slices of bacon
- 4 lettuce leaves
- 2 ripe tomatoes, finely diced
- Mayonnaise
- Sea salt and pepper as desired

Preparation Process

1. Set the temperature of your Ninja Air Fryer to 350°F (175°C).
2. Lay out the bacon slices in the air fryer rack, ensuring they don't overlap.
3. Air fry the bacon for 5-6 Min until crispy, turning once.
4. While the bacon cooks, toast the bread slices.
5. Assemble the sandwiches: Spread mayonnaise on each slice of bread. Layer lettuce, tomato slices, and crispy bacon. Season with Sea salt and pepper.
6. Cut the sandwiches in half and serve.

Serving Total

- Kcal:370 kcal
- Carbs: 26g
- Fat: 25g
- Protein: 12g

24. Mediterranean Falafel Wrap

- Preparation Period: 20 Min
- Cooking Period: 10 Min
- Serves:4

Ingredients needed:

- 8 store-bought or homemade falafel balls
- 4 whole-grain tortillas
- 200g of (240g) hummus
- 1 cucumber, finely diced
- 200g of (150g) cherry tomatoes, halved
- 1/2 red onion, finely diced
- Fresh parsley, diced
- Lemon wedges

Preparation Process

1. Set the temperature of your Ninja Air Fryer to 375°F (190°C).
2. Put the falafel balls in the air fryer rack and cook for 8-10 Min until crispy and heated through.

3. While the falafel cooks, warm the tortillas in a dry frypan or microwave.
4. Spread hummus over each tortilla.
5. Divide the cucumber slices, cherry tomatoes, red onion, and cooked falafel among the tortillas.
6. Sprinkle with fresh parsley and squeeze lemon juice over the filling.
7. Fold in the sides of the tortilla and roll up to create a wrap. Slice in half and serve.

Serving Total

- Kcal:420 kcal
- Carbs: 50g
- Fat: 17g
- Protein: 18g

25. Zesty Buffalo Cauliflower Bites

- Preparation Period: 15 Min
- Cooking Period: 15 Min
- Serves:4

Ingredients needed:

- 1 medium cauliflower, cut into florets
- 50g of (120ml) hot sauce
- 50g of (60g) softened butter
- 5 g of garlic powder
- 5 g of paprika
- 3 g of Sea salt
- 2 g of black pepper
- Ranch or blue cheese dressing for dipping

Preparation Process

1. Set the temperature of your Ninja Air Fryer to 375°F (190°C).
2. In a dish, combine hot sauce, softened butter, garlic powder, paprika, Sea salt, and black pepper.
3. Dip each cauliflower floret into the sauce mixture to coat evenly.

4. Put the coated cauliflower in the air fryer rack in a single layer, ensuring they don't touch.
5. Air fry for 12-15 Min until the cauliflower is crispy and cooked through.
6. Serve with ranch or blue cheese dressing for dipping.

Serving Total

- Kcal:210 kcal
- Carbs: 10g
- Fat: 18g
- Protein: 3g

26. Teriyaki Salmon Dish

- Preparation Period: 15 Min
- Cooking Period: 10 Min
- Serves:2

Ingredients needed:

- 2 salmon fillets
- 50g of (60ml) teriyaki sauce
- 2 cups cooked brown rice
- 200g of broccoli florets, steamed
- 1 carrot, finely diced
- 1/2 cucumber, finely diced
- Sesame seeds for garnish
- Green onions, diced, for garnish

Preparation Process

1. Set the temperature of your Ninja Air Fryer to 375°F (190°C).
2. Brush the salmon fillets with teriyaki sauce.
3. Put the salmon fillets in the air fryer rack.
4. Air fry for 8-10 Min until the salmon is cooked through and flakes easily with a fork.
5. While the salmon cooks, prepare the dish s: Divide cooked brown rice between two dish s. Top with steamed broccoli, carrot slices, and cucumber slices.

6. Put the cooked teriyaki salmon on top.
7. Garnish with sesame seeds and diced green onions.
8. Serve hot.

Serving Total

- Kcal:500 kcal
- Carbs: 48g
- Fat: 15g
- Protein: 40g

27. Spinach and Feta Stuffed Mushrooms

- Preparation Period: 15 Min
- Cooking Period: 10 Min
- Serves:4

Ingredients needed:

- 16 huge mushrooms, cleaned and stems removed
- 200g of (240g) fresh spinach, diced
- 50g of (75g) crumbled feta cheese
- 2 cloves garlic, crushed
- 10g of olive oil
- Sea salt and pepper as desired
- Fresh parsley, diced, for garnish

Preparation Process

1. Set the temperature of your Ninja Air Fryer to 375°F (190°C).
2. In a frypan, heat olive oil over medium heat. Sauté crushed garlic and diced spinach until wilted. Season with Sea salt and pepper.
3. In a dish, mix the sautéed spinach and crumbled feta cheese.
4. Stuff each mushroom cap with the spinach and feta mixture.
5. Put the stuffed mushrooms in the air fryer rack.
6. Air fry for 8-10 Min until the mushrooms are tender and the filling is golden.
7. Garnish with diced fresh parsley before serving.

Serving Total

- Kcal:150 kcal
- Carbs: 6g
- Fat: 11g
- Protein: 6g

28. BBQ Pulled Pork Sliders

- Preparation Period: 10 Min
- Cooking Period: 20 Min
- Serves:6

Ingredients needed:

- 1 pound (450g) pulled pork
- 50g of (120ml) BBQ sauce
- 12 slider buns
- Coleslaw (store-bought or homemade) for topping
- Pickles for garnish

Preparation Process

1. In a dish , mix the pulled pork and BBQ sauce until well coated.
2. Set the temperature of your Ninja Air Fryer to 350°F (175°C).
3. Split the slider buns and put the bottom halves in the air fryer rack.
4. Top each bun with a portion of the BBQ pulled pork.
5. Air fry for 4-5 Min until the buns are toasted and the pork is heated.
6. Remove from the air fryer and top with coleslaw and pickles.
7. Put the top halves of the buns on each slider.
8. Serve warm.

Serving Total

- Kcal:380 kcal
- Carbs: 42g
- Fat: 14g
- Protein: 18g

29. Sweet Potato Fries

- Preparation Period: 10 Min
- Cooking Period: 20 Min
- Serves: 4

Ingredients needed:

- 2 huge sweet potatoes, cut into fries
- 10g of olive oil
- 5 g of paprika
- 3 g of garlic powder
- Sea salt and pepper as desired

Preparation Process

1. Set the temperature of your Ninja Air Fryer to 375°F (190°C).
2. In a dish, toss sweet potato fries with olive oil, paprika, garlic powder, Sea salt, and pepper until evenly coated.
3. Put the seasoned sweet potato fries in the air fryer rack in a single layer.
4. Air fry for 15-20 Min, shaking the rack occasionally, until the fries are crispy and golden.
5. Serve hot as a delicious side dish or snack.

Serving Total

- Kcal: 190 kcal
- Carbs: 28g
- Fat: 8g
- Protein: 2g

30. Caprese Panini

- Preparation Period: 15 Min
- Cooking Period: 5 Min
- Serves: 2

Ingredients needed:

- 4 slices of ciabatta or Italian bread
- 4 slices of mozzarella cheese
- 2 huge tomatoes, finely diced
- Fresh basil leaves
- Balsamic glaze (store-bought or homemade)
- Olive oil for brushing

Preparation Process

1. Set the temperature of your Ninja Air Fryer to 350°F (175°C).
2. Assemble the panini: Layer mozzarella cheese, tomato slices, and fresh basil leaves between slices of bread. Drizzle with balsamic glaze.
3. Brush the outsides of the panini with olive oil.
4. Put the panini in the air fryer rack.
5. Air fry for 4-5 Min until the bread is toasted, and the cheese is softened.
6. Remove, slice, and serve immediately.

Serving Total

- Kcal:380 kcal
- Carbs: 32g
- Fat: 18g
- Protein: 20g

31. Southwest Quinoa Salad

- Preparation Period: 15 Min
- Cooking Period: 15 Min (for quinoa)
- Serves:4

Ingredients needed:

- 200g of quinoa
- 2 cups water
- 1 can (15 oz) black beans, drained and rinsed
- 200g of corn kernels (fresh, frozen, or canned)
- 1 red bell pepper, diced

- 1/2 red onion, finely diced
- 200g of cherry tomatoes, halved
- 50g of fresh cilantro, diced
- Juice of 2 limes
- 10g of olive oil
- 5 g of cumin
- Sea salt and pepper as desired
- Avocado slices for garnish (optional)

Preparation Process

1. Quinoa should be rinsed in cold water and drained.
2. Quinoa and water are combined in a pan. When the quinoa is cooked and the water has been absorbed, bring to a boil, then lower the heat, cover the pot, and simmer for 15 minutes. Observe cooling.
3. Cooked quinoa, black beans, corn, sliced red onion, diced bell pepper, and cherry tomatoes should all be combined in a large plate.
4. Stir together lime juice, cumin, olive oil, sea salt, and pepper in a separate small plate.
5. Over the quinoa mixture, drizzle the dressing and stir to incorporate.
6. Fresh cilantro should be added to the salad just before serving, and avocado slices can be added as a garnish if preferred.

Serving Total

- Kcal:340 kcal
- Carbs: 54g
- Fat: 9g
- Protein: 11g

32. Teriyaki Chicken Rice Dish

- Preparation Period: 10 Min
- Cooking Period: 20 Min
- Serves:4

Ingredients needed:

- 2 Chicken breasts without bones and skin
- 50g of teriyaki sauce
- 2 cups cooked white rice
- 200g of broccoli florets, steamed
- 200g of diced bell peppers (assorted colors)
- 50g of diced green onions
- Sesame seeds for garnish
- Diced red chili peppers for garnish (optional)

Preparation Process

1. Set the temperature of your Ninja Air Fryer to 375°F (190°C).
2. Brush chicken breasts with teriyaki sauce.
3. Put the chicken breasts in the air fryer rack.
4. Air fry for 15-20 Min, turning halfway, until the chicken is cooked through.
5. Let the chicken rest for a few Min before slicing it.
6. While the chicken cooks, prepare the dish s: Divide cooked white rice between four dish s.
7. Top with diced chicken, steamed broccoli florets, diced bell peppers, and green onions.
8. Garnish with sesame seeds and diced red chili peppers if you like it spicy.

Serving Total

- Kcal:360 kcal
- Carbs: 54g
- Fat: 5g
- Protein: 28g

33. Crispy Eggplant Parmesan

- Preparation Period: 20 Min
- Cooking Period: 15 Min
- Serves:4

Ingredients needed:

- 2 huge eggplants, cut into rounds
- 2 cups breadcrumbs
- 200g of crushed Parmesan cheese
- 2 eggs
- 200g of marinara sauce
- 1 1/2 cups diced mozzarella cheese
- Fresh basil leaves for garnish
- Sea salt and pepper as desired

Preparation Process

1. Set the temperature of your Ninja Air Fryer to 375°F (190°C).
2. In a dish, whisk the eggs with a pinch of Sea salt and pepper.
3. In another dish, combine breadcrumbs and crushed Parmesan cheese.
4. Dip each eggplant round into the beaten eggs, allowing excess to drip off, then coat with the breadcrumb mixture.
5. Put the breaded eggplant rounds in the air fryer rack in a single layer.
6. Air fry for 10-15 Min until the eggplant is crispy and golden.
7. Remove the eggplant rounds and top each one with a spoonful of marinara sauce and diced mozzarella cheese.
8. Return them to the air fryer for another 2-3 Min or until the cheese is softened and bubbly.
9. Garnish with fresh basil leaves and serve.

Serving Total

- Kcal:340 kcal
- Carbs: 40g
- Fat: 14g
- Protein: 15g

34. Thai-Inspired Peanut Noodles

- Preparation Period: 15 Min
- Cooking Period: 10 Min (for noodles)
- Serves:4

Ingredients needed:

- 8 oz rice noodles
- 50g of peanut butter
- 50g of soy sauce
- 10g of rice vinegar
- 10g of honey
- 2 cloves garlic, crushed
- 5 g of ginger, crushed
- 3 g of red pepper flakes (adjust to taste)
- 200g of diced bell peppers (assorted colors)
- 200g of diced carrots
- 50g of diced scallions
- Diced peanuts and fresh cilantro for garnish

Preparation Process

1. Cook rice noodles according to package instructions, then drain and rinse with cold water.
2. In a dish, whisk together peanut butter, soy sauce, rice vinegar, honey, crushed garlic, crushed ginger, and red pepper flakes to make the sauce.
3. In a huge dish, combine the cooked rice noodles, diced bell peppers, diced carrots, and diced scallions.
4. Pour the peanut sauce over the noodles and toss to coat.
5. Serve the peanut noodles garnished with diced peanuts and fresh cilantro.

Serving Total

- Kcal:420 kcal
- Carbs: 68g
- Fat: 13g
- Protein: 10g

35. BBQ Grilled Cheese Sandwich

- Preparation Period: 10 Min
- Cooking Period: 5 Min
- Serves:2

Ingredients needed:

- 4 slices of bread
- 4 slices cheddar cheese
- 50g of diced BBQ chicken (leftover or store-bought)
- 10g of butter, softened
- BBQ sauce for dipping (optional)

Preparation Process

1. Set the temperature of your Ninja Air Fryer to 350°F (175°C).
2. Lay out two slices of bread and top each with a slice of cheddar cheese.
3. Divide the diced BBQ chicken between the sandwiches, placing it on top of the cheese.
4. Top each sandwich with another slice of cheddar cheese and the remaining slices of bread.
5. Spread softened butter on the outside of each sandwich.
6. Put the sandwiches in the air fryer rack.
7. Air fry for 3-4 Min on each side until the bread is golden and the cheese is softened.
8. Let them cool for a minute before slicing.
9. Serve with BBQ sauce for dipping if desired.

Serving Total

- Kcal:480 kcal
- Carbs: 40g
- Fat: 30g
- Protein: 18g

36. Lemon Garlic Shrimp Pasta

- Preparation Period: 15 Min
- Cooking Period: 10 Min (for pasta and shrimp)
- Serves:4

Ingredients needed:

- 8 oz linguine or spaghetti

- 1 pound huge shrimp, stripped and deveined
- 4 cloves garlic, crushed
- Zest and juice of 1 lemon
- 10g of olive oil
- 3 g of red pepper flakes (adjust to taste)
- 50g of fresh parsley, diced
- Sea salt and pepper as desired
- Crushed Parmesan cheese for garnish

Preparation Process

1. Cook pasta according to package instructions, then drain and set aside.
2. In a huge dish, toss shrimp with crushed garlic, lemon zest, red pepper flakes, Sea salt, and pepper.
3. Set the temperature of your Ninja Air Fryer to 375°F (190°C).
4. Put the seasoned shrimp in the air fryer rack.
5. Air fry for 6-8 Min until the shrimp are pink and cooked through.
6. In a huge frypan, heat olive oil over medium heat. Add cooked pasta and lemon juice, tossing to combine.
7. Add the cooked shrimp and diced parsley to the pasta, tossing gently.
8. Serve hot with crushed Parmesan cheese for garnish.

Serving Total

- Kcal:410 kcal
- Carbs: 49g
- Fat: 10g
- Protein: 30g

37. Veggie Packed Fried Rice

- Preparation Period: 15 Min
- Cooking Period: 10 Min
- Serves:4

Ingredients needed:

- 2 cups cooked and cooled rice (white or brown)

- 10g of vegetable oil
- 200g of diced carrots
- 200g of frozen peas, thawed
- 200g of diced bell peppers (assorted colors)
- 50g of diced onion
- 2 cloves garlic, crushed
- 2 eggs, beaten
- 3 tablespoons soy sauce
- 5 g of sesame oil
- 50g of diced green onions for garnish
- Sesame seeds for garnish

Preparation Process

1. Set the temperature of your Ninja Air Fryer to 375°F (190°C).
2. Heat vegetable oil in a huge frypan or wok over medium-high heat.
3. Add diced carrots, bell peppers, and diced onion. Stir-fry for 2-3 Min until slightly softened.
4. Push the vegetables to one side of the frypan and add crushed garlic to the other side. Stir-fry for 30 seconds until fragrant.
5. Push the garlic to the side and pour beaten eggs into the empty space. Scramble the eggs until cooked through.
6. Add the cooked and cooled rice, thawed peas, soy sauce, and sesame oil to the frypan. Stir-fry for 3-4 Min, breaking up any clumps of rice.
7. Transfer the fried rice to the air fryer rack and spread it out evenly.
8. Air fry for 3-4 Min until the rice is heated through and slightly crispy.
9. Garnish with diced green onions and sesame seeds before serving.

Serving Total

- Kcal:340 kcal
- Carbs: 52g
- Fat: 10g
- Protein: 11g

38. Hawaiian BBQ Chicken Pizza

- Preparation Period: 15 Min
- Cooking Period: 10 Min
- Serves: 4

Ingredients needed:

- 1 store-bought pizza dough
- 50g of BBQ sauce
- 2 cups cooked and diced chicken breast
- 200g of diced mozzarella cheese
- 50g of diced pineapple
- 50g of diced red onion
- Fresh cilantro leaves for garnish

Preparation Process

1. Set the temperature of your Ninja Air Fryer to 375°F (190°C).
2. Roll out the pizza dough on a floured surface to your desired thickness.
3. Transfer the rolled-out dough to the air fryer rack.
4. Spread BBQ sauce over the pizza dough, leaving a border for the crust.
5. Evenly distribute diced chicken, diced mozzarella cheese, diced pineapple, and diced red onion over the sauce.
6. Air fry for 8-10 Min until the crust is golden and the cheese is softened and bubbly.
7. Garnish with fresh cilantro leaves before serving.

Serving Total

- Kcal: 410 kcal
- Carbs: 48g
- Fat: 14g
- Protein: 25g

39. Creamy Tomato Basil Soup

- Preparation Period: 15 Min
- Cooking Period: 20 Min
- Serves: 4

Ingredients needed:

- 1 can (28 oz) crushed tomatoes
- 200g of vegetable broth
- 50g of heavy cream
- 50g of fresh basil leaves, diced
- 2 cloves garlic, crushed
- 1 small onion, diced
- 10g of olive oil
- Sea salt and pepper as desired
- Crushed Parmesan cheese for garnish
- Croutons for garnish (optional)

Preparation Process

1. In a huge saucepan, heat olive oil over medium heat. Add diced onion and crushed garlic. Sauté for 2-3 Min until softened and fragrant.
2. Add crushed tomatoes, vegetable broth, and diced basil leaves to the saucepan. Season with Sea salt and pepper.
3. Bring the mixture to a boil, then reduce heat and simmer for 15-20 Min, stirring occasionally.
4. Transfer the tomato soup to a blender and puree until smooth. Alternatively, use an immersion blender directly in the saucepan.
5. Return the pureed soup to the saucepan and stir in heavy cream.
6. Heat the soup over low heat, stirring until warmed through.
7. Serve hot, garnished with crushed Parmesan cheese and croutons if desired.

Serving Total

- Kcal:280 kcal
- Carbs: 20g
- Fat: 21g
- Protein: 4g

40. Spicy Buffalo Cauliflower Tacos

- Preparation Period: 20 Min
- Cooking Period: 20 Min

- Serves: 4

Ingredients needed:

- 1 head cauliflower, cut into florets
- 50g of buffalo sauce
- 50g of softened butter
- 200g of diced lettuce
- 200g of diced tomatoes
- 50g of diced red onion
- 50g of crumbled blue cheese (optional)
- 8 small taco-sized flour tortillas
- Ranch or blue cheese dressing for drizzling

Preparation Process

1. Set the temperature of your Ninja Air Fryer to 375°F (190°C).
2. In a dish, whisk together buffalo sauce and softened butter.
3. Dip each cauliflower floret into the buffalo sauce mixture to coat evenly.
4. Put the coated cauliflower in the air fryer rack.
5. Air fry for 15-20 Min until the cauliflower is crispy and cooked through.
6. While the cauliflower cooks, warm the tortillas in a dry frypan or microwave.
7. Assemble the tacos: Fill each tortilla with diced lettuce, diced tomatoes, diced red onion, and crispy buffalo cauliflower.
8. Sprinkle crumbled blue cheese over the top and drizzle with ranch or blue cheese dressing if desired.

Serving Total

- Kcal: 350 kcal
- Carbs: 34g
- Fat: 17g
- Protein: 10g

41. Vegetarian Stuffed Bell Peppers

- Preparation Period: 20 Min
- Cooking Period: 25 Min

- Serves:4

Ingredients needed:

- 4 huge bell peppers, any color
- 200g of cooked quinoa
- 1 can (15 oz) black beans, drained and rinsed
- 200g of corn kernels (fresh, frozen, or canned)
- 200g of diced tomatoes
- 50g of diced cheddar cheese
- 3 g of chili powder
- 3 g of cumin
- Sea salt and pepper as desired
- Fresh cilantro leaves for garnish

Preparation Process

1. Set the temperature of your Ninja Air Fryer to 375°F (190°C).
2. Cut the tops off the bell peppers and remove the seeds and membranes.
3. In a dish, mix cooked quinoa, black beans, corn kernels, diced tomatoes, diced cheddar cheese, chili powder, cumin, Sea salt, and pepper.
4. Stuff each bell pepper with the quinoa and vegetable mixture.
5. Put the stuffed bell peppers in the air fryer rack.
6. Air fry for 20-25 Min until the bell peppers are tender and slightly charred.
7. Garnish with fresh cilantro leaves before serving.

Serving Total

- Kcal:300 kcal
- Carbs: 54g
- Fat: 5g
- Protein: 14g

42. Chicken Fajita Quesadillas

- Preparation Period: 15 Min
- Cooking Period: 10 Min
- Serves:4

Ingredients needed:

- 2 Chicken breasts without bones and skin
- 5 g of chili powder
- 5 g of cumin
- 3 g of paprika
- 3 g of garlic powder
- Sea salt and pepper as desired
- 1 red bell pepper, finely diced
- 1 green bell pepper, finely diced
- 1 onion, finely diced
- 4 huge flour tortillas
- 2 cups diced Mexican cheese blend
- Sour cream and salsa for dipping

Preparation Process

1. Set the temperature of your Ninja Air Fryer to 375°F (190°C).
2. Season chicken breasts with chili powder, cumin, paprika, garlic powder, Sea salt , and pepper.
3. Put the seasoned chicken breasts in the air fryer rack.
4. Air fry for 12-15 Min, turning halfway, until the chicken is cooked through.
5. Let the chicken rest for a few Min before slicing it.
6. While the chicken cooks, sauté diced red and green bell peppers and finely diced onion in a frypan until softened and slightly caramelized.
7. Lay out a tortilla and sprinkle with diced Mexican cheese blend.
8. Top with diced chicken and sautéed fajita vegetables.
9. Put another tortilla on top and press gently to seal.
10. Set the temperature of your Ninja Air Fryer to 375°F (190°C).
11. Lightly oil the air fryer rack with cooking spray.
12. Carefully put the quesadilla in the air fryer and cook for 3-4 Min on each side until crispy and the cheese is softened .
13. Remove, let it cool for a minute, then slice into wedges and serve with sour cream and salsa for dipping.

Serving Total

- Kcal:420 kcal

- Carbs: 32g
- Fat: 20g
- Protein: 30g

Chapter 7:
Dinner Recipes

43. Crispy Air-Fried Chicken Tenders

- Preparation Period: 15 Min
- Cooking Period: 12 Min
- Serves: 4

Ingredients needed:

- 1 pound chicken tenders
- 200g of breadcrumbs
- 50g of crushed Parmesan cheese
- 5 g of paprika
- 3 g of garlic powder
- Sea salt and pepper as desired
- Cooking spray

Preparation Process

1. Set the temperature of your Ninja Air Fryer to 375°F (190°C).
2. In a shallow dish, mix breadcrumbs, Parmesan cheese, paprika, garlic powder, Sea salt, and pepper.
3. Dip each chicken tender into the breadcrumb mixture, ensuring they are evenly coated.
4. Spray the air fryer rack with cooking spray, then arrange the chicken tenders in a single layer.

5. Air fry for 12 Min, flipping halfway through, or until the tenders are cripsy and cooked through.
6. Serve with your favorite dipping sauce.

Serving Total

- Kcal:320 kcal
- Carbs: 15g
- Fat: 12g
- Protein: 35g

44. Air-Fried Salmon with Lemon-Dill Sauce

- Preparation Period: 10 Min
- Cooking Period: 12 Min
- Serves:2

Ingredients needed:

- 2 salmon fillets
- 1 lemon, diced
- 10g of olive oil
- 5 g of dried dill
- Sea salt and pepper as desired

Preparation Process

1. Set the temperature of your Ninja Air Fryer to 375°F (190°C).
2. Season the salmon fillets with Sea salt, pepper, and dried dill. Drizzle olive oil over them.
3. Put lemon slices on top of the salmon.
4. Put the salmon fillets into the air fryer rack.
5. Air fry for 12 Min or until the salmon is flaky and cooked to your desired doneness.
6. Serve with lemon wedges and your choice of side dishes.

Serving Total

- Kcal:350 kcal
- Carbs: 2g

- Fat: 24g
- Protein: 30g

45. Crispy Air-Fried Vegetable Spring Rolls

- Preparation Period: 20 Min
- Cooking Period: 10 Min
- Serves: 4

Ingredients needed:

- 8 spring roll wrappers
- 2 cups mixed vegetables (carrots, cabbage, bell peppers, and bean sprouts), finely diced
- 5 g of soy sauce
- 5 g of sesame oil
- 3 g of ginger, crushed
- 3 g of garlic, crushed
- Cooking spray

Preparation Process

1. In a dish, combine the diced vegetables, soy sauce, sesame oil, ginger, and garlic.
2. Put a spring roll wrapper on a clean surface, and spoon 2-3 tablespoons of the vegetable mixture onto the wrapper.
3. Roll up the wrapper, tucking in the sides, and seal the edge with a bit of water.
4. Set the temperature of your Ninja Air Fryer to 375°F (190°C).
5. Spray the spring rolls with cooking spray and put them in the air fryer rack.
6. Air fry for 10 Min, flipping halfway through, or until the spring rolls are cripsy and crispy.
7. Serve with a dipping sauce of your choice.

Serving Total

- Kcal: 150 kcal
- Carbs: 25g
- Fat: 3g
- Protein: 5g

46. Air-Fried Honey BBQ Chicken Wings

- Preparation Period: 10 Min
- Cooking Period: 20 Min
- Serves: 4

Ingredients needed:

- 2 pounds chicken wings
- 50g of barbecue sauce
- 10g of honey
- 5 g of olive oil
- Sea salt and pepper as desired

Preparation Process

1. In a dish, mix barbecue sauce, honey, olive oil, Sea salt, and pepper.
2. Toss the chicken wings in the sauce mixture until well coated.
3. Set the temperature of your Ninja Air Fryer to 375°F (190°C).
4. Arrange the chicken wings in one layer in the air fryer rack.
5. Air fry for 20 Min, flipping them halfway through, or until the wings are crispy and cooked through.
6. Serve with extra sauce for dipping.

Serving Total

- Kcal: 420 kcal
- Carbs: 15g
- Fat: 28g
- Protein: 28g

47. Garlic Parmesan Air-Fried Potato Wedges

- Preparation Period: 15 Min
- Cooking Period: 20 Min
- Serves: 4

Ingredients needed:

- 4 huge russet potatoes, cut into wedges
- 10g of olive oil
- 2 cloves garlic, crushed
- 50g of crushed Parmesan cheese
- 5 g of dried rosemary
- Sea salt and pepper as desired

Preparation Process

1. In a huge dish, toss the potato wedges with olive oil, crushed garlic, Parmesan cheese, dried rosemary, Sea salt, and pepper.
2. Set the temperature of your Ninja Air Fryer to 375°F (190°C).
3. Arrange the potato wedges in one layer in the air fryer rack.
4. Air fry for 20 Min or until the wedges are crispy and cripsy, shaking the rack occasionally for even cooking.
5. Serve hot with your favorite dipping sauce.

Serving Total

- Kcal:240 kcal
- Carbs: 35g
- Fat: 9g
- Protein: 4g

48. Crunchy Air-Fried Shrimp Tacos

- Preparation Period: 20 Min
- Cooking Period: 10 Min
- Serves:4

Ingredients needed:

- 1 pound huge shrimp, stripped and deveined
- 200g of panko breadcrumbs
- 2 eggs, beaten
- 5 g of paprika
- 3 g of cayenne pepper

- 8 small tortillas
- 200g of diced lettuce
- 200g of diced tomatoes
- 50g of sour cream
- 50g of diced fresh cilantro
- Lime wedges for serving

Preparation Process

1. In a shallow dish, combine panko breadcrumbs, paprika, and cayenne pepper.
2. Dip each shrimp into beaten eggs, then coat with the breadcrumb mixture.
3. Set the temperature of your Ninja Air Fryer to 375°F (190°C).
4. Arrange the breaded shrimp in one layer in the air fryer rack.
5. Air fry for 10 Min or until the shrimp are golden and crispy.
6. Warm the tortillas in the air fryer for 1-2 Min.
7. Assemble tacos with diced lettuce, diced tomatoes, crispy shrimp, sour cream, and cilantro.
8. Serve with lime wedges for squeezing.

Serving Total

- Kcal:380 kcal
- Carbs: 36g
- Fat: 14g
- Protein: 25g

49. Air-Fried Vegetable Stir-Fry

- Preparation Period: 15 Min
- Cooking Period: 10 Min
- Serves:4

Ingredients needed:

- 2 cups mixed vegetables (bell peppers, broccoli, carrots, snap peas), diced
- 5 g of vegetable oil
- 2 cloves garlic, crushed
- 50g of low-sodium soy sauce

- 5 g of honey
- 5 g of sesame oil
- 5 g of cornstarch mixed with 10g of water
- Cooked rice or noodles for serving

Preparation Process

1. Set the temperature of your Ninja Air Fryer to 375°F (190°C).
2. In a dish, toss the diced vegetables with vegetable oil and crushed garlic.
3. Arrange the vegetables in the air fryer rack.
4. Air fry for 8-10 Min, shaking the rack occasionally, until the vegetables are tender and slightly crispy.
5. In a small saucepan, combine soy sauce, honey, and sesame oil. Heat over low heat, then stir in the cornstarch-water mixture until the sauce thickens.
6. Serve the air-fried vegetables over cooked rice or noodles and drizzle with the sauce.

Serving Total

- Kcal:160 kcal
- Carbs: 25g
- Fat: 5g
- Protein: 5g

50. Air-Fried Beef and Broccoli

- Preparation Period: 20 Min
- Cooking Period: 10 Min
- Serves:4

Ingredients needed:

- 1 pound flank steak, finely diced
- 2 cups broccoli florets
- 50g of low-sodium soy sauce
- 10g of hoisin sauce
- 2 cloves garlic, crushed
- 5 g of crushed ginger

- 5 g of cornstarch mixed with 10g of water
- Cooked rice for serving

Preparation Process

1. In a dish, marinate the diced flank steak with soy sauce, hoisin sauce, crushed garlic, and crushed ginger. Let it sit for 15 Min.
2. Set the temperature of your Ninja Air Fryer to 375°F (190°C).
3. Arrange the marinated steak and broccoli in the air fryer rack.
4. Air fry for 8-10 Min, shaking the rack occasionally, until the beef is cooked and the broccoli is tender.
5. In a small saucepan, heat the cornstarch-water mixture over low heat until it thickens, then drizzle it over the beef and broccoli.
6. Serve hot over cooked rice.

Serving Total

- Kcal:280 kcal
- Carbs: 18g
- Fat: 10g
- Protein: 25g

51. Air-Fried Stuffed Bell Peppers

- Preparation Period: 30 Min
- Cooking Period: 20 Min
- Serves:4

Ingredients needed:

- 4 huge bell peppers, tops removed and seeds removed
- 1 pound crushed beef
- 50g of cooked rice
- 200g of tomato sauce
- 50g of diced cheddar cheese
- 3 g of Italian seasoning
- Sea salt and pepper as desired

Preparation Process

1. In a frypan, cook the crushed beef until browned, then drain any excess fat.
2. In a dish, mix the cooked crushed beef, cooked rice, tomato sauce, diced cheddar cheese, Italian seasoning, Sea salt, and pepper.
3. Set the temperature of your Ninja Air Fryer to 375°F (190°C).
4. Stuff each bell pepper with the beef and rice mixture.
5. Put the stuffed peppers in the air fryer rack.
6. Air fry for 20 Min or until the peppers are tender and the filling is hot and bubbly.
7. Serve hot, garnished with extra cheese if desired.

Serving Total

- Kcal:390 kcal
- Carbs: 28g
- Fat: 22g
- Protein: 22g

52. Air-Fried Veggie Quesadillas

- Preparation Period: 20 Min
- Cooking Period: 10 Min
- Serves:4

Ingredients needed:

- 4 huge flour tortillas
- 200g of diced Mexican cheese blend
- 200g of mixed vegetables (bell peppers, onions, mushrooms), sautéed
- 50g of black beans, drained and rinsed
- 3 g of chili powder
- Cooking spray

Preparation Process

1. Lay out a tortilla and sprinkle one-half with diced cheese, sautéed vegetables, black beans, and chili powder.
2. Fold the other half of the tortilla over the filling to create a half-moon shape.
3. Set the temperature of your Ninja Air Fryer to 375°F (190°C).

4. Spray both sides of the quesadilla with cooking spray.
5. Put the quesadilla in the air fryer rack.
6. Air fry for 5 Min, flip, and air fry for an additional 5 Min or until the quesadilla is cripsy and the cheese is softened .
7. Repeat with the remaining quesadillas.
8. Serve hot with salsa and sour cream.

Serving Total

- Kcal:320 kcal
- Carbs: 40g
- Fat: 12g
- Protein: 14g

53. Air-Fried Teriyaki Chicken Skewers

- Preparation Period: 20 Min
- Cooking Period: 15 Min
- Serves:4

Ingredients needed:

- 1 pound Chicken thighs without bones and skin, cut into cubes
- 50g of teriyaki sauce
- 10g of honey
- 5 g of crushed garlic
- 5 g of crushed ginger
- Wooden skewers, soaked in water

Preparation Process

1. In a dish , mix teriyaki sauce, honey, crushed garlic, and crushed ginger.
2. Thread the chicken cubes onto the soaked wooden skewers.
3. Set the temperature of your Ninja Air Fryer to 375°F (190°C).
4. Brush the chicken skewers with the teriyaki sauce mixture.
5. Arrange the skewers in the air fryer rack.
6. Air fry for 12-15 Min, turning halfway through, or until the chicken is cooked through and has a nice glaze.

7. Serve with steamed rice and your choice of vegetables.

Serving Total

- Kcal:260 kcal
- Carbs: 13g
- Fat: 9g
- Protein: 30g

54. Air-Fried Veggie and Quinoa Stuffed Peppers

- Preparation Period: 30 Min
- Cooking Period: 20 Min
- Serves:4

Ingredients needed:

- 4 huge bell peppers, tops removed and seeds removed
- 200g of cooked quinoa
- 200g of mixed vegetables (zucchini, corn, tomatoes)
- 50g of diced mozzarella cheese
- 3 g of Italian seasoning
- Sea salt and pepper as desired
- Cooking spray

Preparation Process

1. In a dish, combine cooked quinoa, mixed vegetables, diced mozzarella cheese, Italian seasoning, Sea salt, and pepper.
2. Set the temperature of your Ninja Air Fryer to 375°F (190°C).
3. Stuff each bell pepper with the quinoa and vegetable mixture.
4. Put the stuffed peppers in the air fryer rack.
5. Air fry for 20 Min or until the peppers are tender, and the filling is hot and cheesy.
6. If preferred, pour some olive oil on top before serving.

Serving Total

- Kcal:280 kcal
- Carbs: 39g

- Fat: 10g
- Protein: 11g

55. Air-Fried Coconut Shrimp

- Preparation Period: 20 Min
- Cooking Period: 10 Min
- Serves: 4

Ingredients needed:

- 1 pound huge shrimp, stripped and deveined
- 200g of diced coconut
- 200g of panko breadcrumbs
- 2 eggs, beaten
- Cooking spray
- Sweet chili dipping sauce

Preparation Process

1. In separate shallow dishes, put beaten eggs, diced coconut, and panko breadcrumbs.
2. Dip each shrimp into the beaten eggs, then coat with diced coconut and panko breadcrumbs.
3. Set the temperature of your Ninja Air Fryer to 375°F (190°C).
4. Spray the shrimp with cooking spray.
5. Arrange the coated shrimp in one layer in the air fryer rack.
6. Air fry for 8-10 Min or until the shrimp are crispy and cripsy.
7. Serve with sweet chili dipping sauce.

Serving Total

- Kcal: 350 kcal
- Carbs: 16g
- Fat: 20g
- Protein: 23g

56. Air-Fried Sausage and Pepper Hoagies

- Preparation Period: 15 Min
- Cooking Period: 10 Min
- Serves: 4

Ingredients needed:

- 4 Italian sausages
- 2 bell peppers, diced
- 1 onion, diced
- 4 hoagie rolls
- 50g of marinara sauce
- 50g of diced mozzarella cheese
- Olive oil
- Sea salt and pepper as desired

Preparation Process

1. Set the temperature of your Ninja Air Fryer to 375°F (190°C).
2. Brush sausages, diced peppers, and onions with olive oil. Season with Sea salt and pepper.
3. Arrange the sausages, peppers, and onions in the air fryer rack.
4. Air fry for 8-10 Min, turning the sausages and stirring the peppers and onions halfway through, or until the sausages are cooked through and the vegetables are tender.
5. While the sausages and vegetables cook, split the hoagie rolls and toast them in the air fryer for 2-3 Min.
6. Slice the sausages and assemble hoagies with marinara sauce, sautéed peppers and onions, and diced mozzarella cheese.
7. Air fry for an additional 2-3 Min or until the cheese is softened and bubbly.
8. Serve hot.

Serving Total

- Kcal: 480 kcal
- Carbs: 38g
- Fat: 27g

- Protein: 20g

57. Air-Fried Sweet Potato Fries

- Preparation Period: 15 Min
- Cooking Period: 15 Min
- Serves: 4

Ingredients needed:

- 2 huge sweet potatoes, cut into fries
- 10g of olive oil
- 5 g of paprika
- 3 g of garlic powder
- 3 g of cayenne pepper (adjust to taste)
- Sea salt and pepper as desired

Preparation Process

1. In a huge dish, toss sweet potato fries with olive oil, paprika, garlic powder, cayenne pepper, Sea salt, and pepper until evenly coated.
2. Set the temperature of your Ninja Air Fryer to 375°F (190°C).
3. Arrange the seasoned sweet potato fries in one layer in the air fryer rack.
4. Air fry for 12-15 Min, shaking the rack occasionally, or until the fries are crispy and cooked through.
5. Serve hot with your favorite dipping sauce.

Serving Total

- Kcal: 180 kcal
- Carbs: 27g
- Fat: 8g
- Protein: 2g

58. Air-Fried BBQ Pulled Pork Sandwiches

- **Preparation Period:** 15 Min (plus marinating time)
- **Cooking Period:** 20 Min
- **Serves:** 4

Ingredients needed:

- 1 pound pork shoulder or butt, trimmed and cut into chunks
- 50g of barbecue sauce
- 50g of apple cider vinegar
- 5 g of brown sugar
- 5 g of smoked paprika
- 3 g of garlic powder
- 4 hamburger buns
- Coleslaw (optional)

Preparation Process

1. In a dish , combine barbecue sauce, apple cider vinegar, brown sugar, smoked paprika, and garlic powder to make the marinade.
2. Add the pork chunks to the marinade and refrigerate for at least 2 hrs or overnight.
3. Set the temperature of your Ninja Air Fryer to 360°F (180°C).
4. Arrange the marinated pork in the air fryer rack.
5. Air fry for 20 Min, stirring occasionally, until the pork is tender and easily shreds.
6. Shred the pork using forks and mix it with the cooking juices.
7. Toast the hamburger buns in the air fryer for a minute.
8. Assemble sandwiches with the pulled pork and coleslaw if desired.
9. Serve hot.

Serving Total

- Kcal:450 kcal
- Carbs: 48g
- Fat: 14g
- Protein: 30g

59. Air-Fried Cajun Shrimp and Grits

- Preparation Period: 15 Min
- Cooking Period: 15 Min
- Serves:4

Ingredients needed:

- 1 pound huge shrimp, stripped and deveined
- 200g of quick-cooking grits
- 800g of water
- 10g of butter
- 5 g of Cajun seasoning
- Sea salt and pepper as desired
- Diced green onions for garnish

Preparation Process

1. In a medium saucepan, bring 800g of of water to a boil. Stir in the grits and reduce the heat to low. Cook according to the package instructions, adding butter, Cajun seasoning, Sea salt , and pepper while cooking.
2. Set the temperature of your Ninja Air Fryer to 375°F (190°C).
3. Season the shrimp with Cajun seasoning.
4. Arrange the seasoned shrimp in one layer in the air fryer rack.
5. Air fry for 5-7 Min or until the shrimp are pink and cooked through.
6. Serve the Cajun shrimp over a bed of creamy grits, garnished with diced green onions.

Serving Total

- Kcal:350 kcal
- Carbs: 43g
- Fat: 10g
- Protein: 20g

60. Air-Fried Buffalo Cauliflower Bites

- Preparation Period: 15 Min
- Cooking Period: 12 Min
- Serves:4

Ingredients needed:

- 1 head of cauliflower, cut into florets
- 50g of wheat flour

- 50g of water
- 5 g of garlic powder
- 3 g of paprika
- 50g of buffalo sauce
- 10g of butter, softened
- Ranch or blue cheese dressing for dipping

Preparation Process

1. To make the batter, combine the flour, water, paprika, and garlic powder in a bowl.
2. Each cauliflower floret should be dipped into the batter and thoroughly coated.
3. Set the temperature of your Ninja Air Fryer to 375°F (190°C).
4. Arrange the battered cauliflower in one layer in the air fryer rack.
5. Air fry for 12 Min, flipping halfway through, or until the cauliflower is crispy and golden.
6. In a separate dish, mix buffalo sauce and softened butter.
7. Toss the air-fried cauliflower in the buffalo sauce mixture until evenly coated.
8. Serve with ranch or blue cheese dressing for dipping.

Serving Total

- Kcal:160 kcal
- Carbs: 20g
- Fat: 7g
- Protein: 4g

61. Air-Fried Lemon Herb Whole Chicken

- **Preparation Period:** 15 Min (plus marinating time)
- **Cooking Period:** 60 Min
- **Serves:** 4

Ingredients needed:

- 1 whole chicken (3-4 pounds)
- 2 lemons, diced
- 4 cloves of garlic, crushed
- 10g of olive oil

- 5 g of dried rosemary
- 5 g of dried thyme
- Sea salt and pepper as desired

Preparation Process

1. In a dish , combine crushed garlic, olive oil, dried rosemary, dried thyme, Sea salt , and pepper.
2. Rub the chicken inside and out with the garlic and herb mixture. Put lemon slices inside the chicken cavity.
3. Refrigerate the chicken for at least 4 hrs or overnight for marinating.
4. Set the temperature of your Ninja Air Fryer to 360°F (180°C).
5. Put the marinated chicken in the air fryer rack.
6. Air fry for 60 Min or until the chicken's internal temperature reaches 165°F (74°C), flipping it halfway through.
7. Before carving and serving, give the chicken a few min to rest.

Serving Total

- Kcal:350 kcal
- Carbs: 3g
- Fat: 23g
- Protein: 30g

Chapter 8:
Dessert Recipes

---
62. Cinnamon Sugar Donut Holes

- Preparation Period: 10 Min
- Cooking Period: 6 Min
- Serves:4

Ingredients needed:

- 200g of wheat flour
- 50g of sugar
- 5g of leavening
- 3g of crushed cinnamon
- 2g of Sea salt
- 50g of milk
- 5g of vanilla essence
- 1 egg
- 10g of softened butter
- 50g of refined sugar
- 3g of crushed cinnamon

Preparation Process

1. In a mixing dish , whisk together flour, sugar, leavening , cinnamon, and Sea salt .
2. In another dish , combine milk, vanilla essence, egg, and softened butter.
3. Mix only till incorporated after adding the wet components to the dry ones.
4. Set the temperature of your Ninja Air Fryer to 350°F (175°C).
5. Roll dough into 1-inch balls and put them in the air fryer rack.
6. Cook for 6 Min, turning halfway through, until donut holes are cripsy.
7. In a small dish , mix refined sugar and cinnamon.
8. Roll the warm donut holes in the cinnamon-sugar mixture until coated.
9. Serve and enjoy!

Serving Total

- Kcal:242 kcal
- Carbs: 45g
- Fat: 6g
- Protein: 4g

63. Chocolate Lava Cake

- Preparation Period: 15 Min
- Cooking Period: 10 Min
- Serves: 2

Ingredients needed:

- 50g of unSea salt ed butter
- 2 oz of semi-sweet chocolate chips
- 50g of refined sugar
- 1 egg
- 1 egg yolk
- 3g of vanilla essence
- 10g of wheat flour
- Pinch of Sea salt

Preparation Process

1. In a frypan , melt the butter and chocolate chips together.
2. Stir in refined sugar until well combined.
3. Add egg, egg yolk, and vanilla essence; mix until smooth.
4. Fold in flour and a pinch of Sea salt .
5. Set the temperature of your Ninja Air Fryer to 350°F (175°C).
6. Oil two ramekins and pour the batter evenly into them.
7. Put the ramekins in the air fryer rack.
8. Cook for 10 Min until the cakes have a firm edge but are still gooey in the center.
9. Carefully remove, let them cool for a minute, and serve.

Serving Total

- Kcal:498 kcal
- Carbs: 40g
- Fat: 35g
- Protein: 8g

64. Apple Crisp

- Preparation Period: 15 Min
- Cooking Period: 15 Min
- Serves: 4

Ingredients needed:

- 800g of diced apples (stripped and cored)
- 5g of lemon juice
- 50g of rolled oats
- 50g of wheat flour
- 50g of brown sugar
- 50g of processed sugar
- 3g of crushed cinnamon
- 50g of salt-free butter(cubed)

Preparation Process

1. Toss diced apples with lemon juice and put them in an oiled baking dish that fits in the air fryer rack.
2. In a separate dish, combine oats, flour, brown sugar, processed sugar, and cinnamon.
3. Add cubed butter and use a fork to mix until crumbly.
4. Sprinkle the oat mixture evenly over the apples.
5. Set the temperature of your Ninja Air Fryer to 350°F (175°C).
6. Put the baking dish in the air fryer rack.
7. Cook for 15 Min until the topping is golden and the apples are tender.
8. Allow it to cool slightly before serving.

Serving Total

- Kcal: 277 kcal
- Carbs: 50g
- Fat: 8g
- Protein: 2g

65. Blueberry Lemon Muffins

- Preparation Period: 10 Min
- Cooking Period: 12 Min
- Serves: 6

Ingredients needed:

- 200g of wheat flour
- 50g of sugar
- 5g of leavening
- 3g of baking soda
- 2g of Sea salt
- 50g of plain Greek yogurt
- 50g of milk
- 50g of salt-free butter (softened)
- 1 egg
- 5g of lemon zest
- 200g of fresh blueberries

Preparation Process

1. Flour, sugar, leavening, baking soda, and sea salt should be combined in a dish.
2. In another dish, mix yogurt, milk, softened butter, egg, and lemon zest.
3. Combine wet and dry ingredients, then gently fold in blueberries.
4. Set the temperature of your Ninja Air Fryer to 350°F (175°C).
5. Line muffin cups with paper liners.
6. Fill each muffin cup about two-thirds full with batter.
7. Put muffin cups in the air fryer rack.
8. Cook for 12 Min until muffins are golden and a toothpick comes out clean when inserted.
9. Cool before serving.

Serving Total

- Kcal: 245 kcal
- Carbs: 39g
- Fat: 8g

- Protein: 5g

66. Banana Fritters

- Preparation Period: 10 Min
- Cooking Period: 8 Min
- Serves: 4

Ingredients needed:

- 2 ripe bananas (mashed)
- 50g of wheat flour
- 50g of milk
- 10g of sugar
- 3g of leavening
- 2g of vanilla essence
- Pinch of Sea salt
- Oil for spraying

Preparation Process

1. In a dish, combine mashed bananas, flour, milk, sugar, leavening, vanilla essence, and a pinch of Sea salt. Mix until smooth.
2. Set the temperature of your Ninja Air Fryer to 350°F (175°C).
3. Drop spoonfuls of the batter onto an oiled air fryer tray.
4. Spray the tops with a light coating of oil.
5. Cook for 8 Min until fritters are cripsy and cooked through.
6. Serve warm.

Serving Total

- Kcal: 149 kcal
- Carbs: 33g
- Fat: 1g
- Protein: 2g

67. Strawberry Shortcake

- Preparation Period: 15 Min
- Cooking Period: 5 Min
- Serves: 4

Ingredients needed:

- 200g of strawberries (diced)
- 10g of sugar
- 200g of wheat flour
- 50g of sugar
- 2g of Sea salt
- 5g of leavening
- 2g of baking soda
- 50g of salt-free butter (cold and cubed)
- 50g of buttermilk
- Whipped cream for topping

Preparation Process

1. In a dish, combine diced strawberries and 10g of of sugar. Set aside to macerate.
2. In another dish, whisk together flour, 50g of sugar, Sea salt, leavening, and baking soda.
3. Add cold, cubed butter to the dry ingredients and use a pastry cutter or fork to cut it into the mixture until crumbly.
4. Pour in buttermilk and mix until a dough forms.
5. Set the temperature of your Ninja Air Fryer to 350°F (175°C).
6. Shape the dough into shortcakes by dividing it into four equal pieces.
7. Put the shortcakes in the air fryer rack.
8. Cook for 5 Min until they are crispy.
9. Slice the shortcakes in half horizontally and layer with macerated strawberries and whipped cream.
10. Serve immediately.

Serving Total

- Kcal: 310 kcal

- Carbs: 53g
- Fat: 9g
- Protein: 4g

68. Raspberry Chocolate Turnovers

- Preparation Period: 15 Min
- Cooking Period: 10 Min
- Serves: 4

Ingredients needed:

- 1 sheet puff pastry (thawed)
- 50g of fresh raspberries
- 2 oz semi-sweet chocolate chips
- 10g of refined sugar (for dusting)

Preparation Process

1. Roll out the thawed puff pastry and cut it into four equal squares.
2. Put raspberries and chocolate chips in the center of each square.
3. Fold the pastry over to form a triangle and seal the edges by pressing with a fork.
4. Set the temperature of your Ninja Air Fryer to 350°F (175°C).
5. Put the turnovers in the air fryer rack.
6. Cook for 10 Min until they are golden and puffed.
7. Dust with refined sugar before serving.

Serving Total

- Kcal: 264 kcal
- Carbs: 29g
- Fat: 15g
- Protein: 4g

69. Peach Cobbler

- Preparation Period: 15 Min
- Cooking Period: 15 Min
- Serves: 6

Ingredients needed:

- 800g of canned or fresh peaches (diced)
- 50g of sugar
- 5g of vanilla essence
- 50g of wheat flour
- 50g of sugar
- 5g of leavening
- 2g of Sea salt
- 50g of milk
- 50g of salt-free butter (softened)

Preparation Process

1. In a dish, combine peaches, sugar, and vanilla essence. Set aside.
2. In another dish, whisk together flour, sugar, leavening, and Sea salt.
3. Stir in milk and softened butter until the batter is smooth.
4. Set the temperature of your Ninja Air Fryer to 350°F (175°C).
5. Pour the peach mixture into an oiled baking dish that fits in the air fryer rack.
6. Drop spoonfuls of batter over the peaches.
7. Cook for 15 Min until the cobbler is cripsy and bubbling.
8. Let it cool slightly before serving.

Serving Total

- Kcal:330 kcal
- Carbs: 66g
- Fat: 7g
- Protein: 3g

70. Peanut Butter Chocolate Cookies

- Preparation Period: 10 Min
- Cooking Period: 6 Min
- Serves:8

Ingredients needed:

- 50g of peanut butter

- 50g of sugar
- 50g of brown sugar
- 50g of wheat flour
- 50g of cocoa powder
- 3g of baking soda
- 2g of Sea salt
- 1 egg
- 3g of vanilla essence
- 50g of chocolate chips

Preparation Process

1. Peanut butter, sugar, and brown sugar should be blended together in a dish.
2. Add egg and vanilla essence; mix until well combined.
3. In another dish, whisk together flour, cocoa powder, baking soda, and Sea salt.
4. Combine wet and dry ingredients, then fold in chocolate chips.
5. Set the temperature of your Ninja Air Fryer to 350°F (175°C).
6. Drop spoonfuls of cookie dough onto an oiled air fryer tray.
7. Flatten each cookie slightly with a fork.
8. Cook for 6 Min until cookies are set.
9. Allow them to cool before serving.

Serving Total

- Kcal:263 kcal
- Carbs: 34g
- Fat: 13g
- Protein: 6g

71. Churros with Chocolate Sauce

- Preparation Period: 15 Min
- Cooking Period: 10 Min
- Serves:4

Ingredients needed:

- 200g of water

- 2 1/10g of sugar
- 3g of Sea salt
- 10g of vegetable oil
- 200g of wheat flour
- 3g of crushed cinnamon
- 50g of sugar (for coating)
- Vegetable oil for frying
- 4 oz semi-sweet chocolate (for sauce)
- 50g of heavy cream (for sauce)

Preparation Process

1. In a saucepan, combine water, sugar, Sea salt, and 10g of of vegetable oil. Bring to a boil.
2. Remove from heat and add flour and cinnamon. Stir until it forms a smooth dough.
3. Set the temperature of your Ninja Air Fryer to 375°F (190°C).
4. Fill a piping bag with the dough and pipe strips into the air fryer rack.
5. Cook for 10 Min until churros are cripsy and crispy.
6. In the meantime, prepare the chocolate sauce by melting chocolate and heavy cream together in a microwave-safe dish, stirring until smooth.
7. Once churros are cooked, immediately roll them in a mixture of sugar and cinnamon.
8. Serve churros with the chocolate sauce for dipping.

Serving Total

- Kcal:429 kcal
- Carbs: 50g
- Fat: 23g
- Protein: 4g

72. Chocolate-Dipped Strawberries

- Preparation Period: 15 Min
- Cooking Period: 2 Min (chocolate melting)
- Serves:4

Ingredients needed:

- 200g of fresh strawberries (washed and dried)
- 4 oz semi-sweet chocolate chips
- 5g of coconut oil (optional, for smoother chocolate)

Preparation Process

1. In a dish that can be microwaved, place the chocolate chips and, if using, the coconut oil.
2. Stirring in between, microwave in 30-second intervals until the chocolate is totally softened and smooth.
3. Dip each strawberry into the softened chocolate, coating it halfway.
4. Put the dipped strawberries on a parchment paper-lined tray.
5. Allow them to cool and harden for about 10 Min before serving.

Serving Total

- Kcal:107 kcal
- Carbs: 16g
- Fat: 5g
- Protein: 1g

73. Mini Apple Pies

- Preparation Period: 20 Min
- Cooking Period: 10 Min
- Serves:6

Ingredients needed:

- 2 cups diced apples (stripped and cored)
- 50g of sugar
- 3g of crushed cinnamon
- 3g of lemon juice
- 5g of cornstarch
- one sheet of puff pastry (thawed)
- 1 egg (beaten, for egg wash)
- 5g of refined sugar (for dusting)

Preparation Process

1. In a dish , mix diced apples, sugar, cinnamon, lemon juice, and cornstarch until well combined.
2. Roll out the puff pastry and cut it into six equal squares.
3. Spoon the apple mixture onto each square.
4. Fold the pastry over the filling to form a triangle and seal the edges with a fork.
5. Set the temperature of your Ninja Air Fryer to 350°F (175°C).
6. Brush the tops of the pies with beaten egg.
7. Put the pies in the air fryer rack.
8. Cook for 10 Min until the pies are cripsy.
9. Dust with refined sugar before serving.

Serving Total

- Kcal:236 kcal
- Carbs: 38g
- Fat: 9g
- Protein: 2g

74. Pumpkin Spice Bites

- Preparation Period: 15 Min
- Cooking Period: 6 Min
- Serves:4

Ingredients needed:

- 200g of canned pumpkin puree
- 50g of brown sugar
- 50g of processed sugar
- 5g of pumpkin pie spice
- 5g of vanilla essence
- 1 egg
- 200g of wheat flour
- 3g of leavening
- 2g of baking soda
- Pinch of Sea salt

- Refined sugar for dusting

Preparation Process

1. In a dish, combine pumpkin puree, brown sugar, processed sugar, pumpkin pie spice, vanilla essence, and egg.
2. In another dish, whisk together flour, leavening, baking soda, and a pinch of Sea salt.
3. Add the dry ingredients to the wet ingredients and mix until well combined.
4. Set the temperature of your Ninja Air Fryer to 350°F (175°C).
5. Drop spoonfuls of the batter onto an oiled air fryer tray.
6. Cook for 6 Min until the bites are cooked through and have a golden color.
7. Dust with refined sugar before serving.

Serving Total

- Kcal:229 kcal
- Carbs: 52g
- Fat: 1g
- Protein: 4g

75. Lemon Bars

- Preparation Period: 20 Min
- Cooking Period: 20 Min
- Serves:9

Ingredients needed:

- 200g of wheat flour
- 50g of salt-free butter(softened)
- 50g of refined sugar
- 2 huge eggs
- 200g of processed sugar
- 10g of wheat flour
- 10g of lemon juice
- 3g of lemon zest
- 2g of leavening

- Refined sugar for dusting

Preparation Process

1. In a dish, mix 200g of flour, softened butter, and 50g of refined sugar until it forms a dough.
2. Press the dough into the bottom of an oiled baking dish that fits in the air fryer rack.
3. Set the temperature of your Ninja Air Fryer to 325°F (160°C).
4. Bake the crust for 10 Min.
5. While the crust is baking, beat eggs, processed sugar, 10g of flour, lemon juice, lemon zest, and leavening together until well combined.
6. Pour the lemon mixture over the partially baked crust.
7. Cook for an additional 10 Min until the filling is set.
8. Allow it to cool completely before cutting into squares and dusting with refined sugar.

Serving Total

- Kcal:240 kcal
- Carbs: 35g
- Fat: 10g
- Protein: 2g

76. Coconut Macaroons

- Preparation Period: 15 Min
- Cooking Period: 10 Min
- Serves:12

Ingredients needed:

- 2 2/3 cups sweetened diced coconut
- 1/3 cup wheat flour
- 2g of Sea salt
- 2/3 cup sweetened condensed milk
- 5g of vanilla essence
- 2 huge egg whites

- 50g of semi-sweet chocolate chips (optional, for drizzling)

Preparation Process

1. In a dish, combine diced coconut, flour, and Sea salt.
2. Add sweetened condensed milk and vanilla essence; mix until well combined.
3. Egg whites should be beaten until stiff peaks form in a separate bowl.
4. Gently fold the egg whites into the coconut mixture after beating them.
5. Set the temperature of your Ninja Air Fryer to 350°F (175°C).
6. Drop spoonful of the mixture onto the oiled air fryer tray.
7. Cook for 10 Min until the macaroons are crispy.
8. Allow them to cool.
9. If desired, melt chocolate chips and drizzle over the macaroons.

Serving total

- Kcal:192 kcal
- Carbs: 25g
- Fat: 10g
- Protein: 2g

77. Rice Krispies Treats

- Preparation Period: 10 Min
- Cooking Period: 2 Min (melting marshmallow mixture)
- Serves:8

Ingredients needed:

- 3 tbsp salt free butter
- 800g of miniature marshmallows
- 6 cups Rice Krispies cereal

Preparation Process

1. In a frypan, melt the butter and marshmallows together in 30-second intervals, stirring in between, until smooth.
2. Stir in the Rice Krispies cereal until well coated.
3. Set the temperature of your Ninja Air Fryer to 350°F (175°C).

4. Oil a baking dish that fits in the air fryer rack.
5. Press the mixture into the baking dish.
6. Cook for 2 Min until the mixture is set.
7. Allow it to cool before cutting into squares.

Serving Total

- Kcal:170 kcal
- Carbs: 38g
- Fat: 2g
- Protein: 1g

78. Chocolate Peanut Butter Banana Bites

- Preparation Period: 15 Min
- Cooking Period: 8 Min
- Serves:4

Ingredients needed:

- 2 ripe bananas (cut into rounds)
- 10g of peanut butter
- 50g of semi-sweet chocolate chips

Preparation Process

1. Spread peanut butter on half of the banana rounds and top with the remaining halves.
2. Set the temperature of your Ninja Air Fryer to 350°F (175°C).
3. Put the banana sandwiches in the air fryer rack.
4. Cook for 8 Min until they are warm and slightly crispy.
5. Melt the chocolate chips in a microwave-safe dish.
6. Drizzle the softened chocolate over the banana bites.
7. Let them cool before serving.

Serving Total

- Kcal:170 kcal
- Carbs: 28g

- Fat: 7g
- Protein: 2g

79. Mixed Berry Parfait

- Preparation Period: 15 Min
- Cooking Period: 0 Min
- Serves: 4

Ingredients needed:

- 2 cups mixed berries (strawberries, blueberries, raspberries)
- 50g of granola
- 200g of Greek yogurt
- 10g of honey

Preparation Process

1. Wash and prepare the mixed berries.
2. In serving glasses or dish s, layer Greek yogurt, mixed berries, granola, and a drizzle of honey.
3. Repeat the layers as desired.
4. Serve immediately.

Serving Total

- Kcal: 180 kcal
- Carbs: 36g
- Fat: 2g
- Protein: 8g

80. Chia Pudding Parfait

- Preparation Period: 5 Min
- Cooking Period: 0 Min (needs to refrigerate)
- Serves: 1

Ingredients needed:

- 2 tbsps. Full of chia seeds

- 1/2 C. full of almond milk
- 1/2 C. full of Greek yogurt
- 1/2 C. full of mixed berries (strawberries, blueberries, raspberries)
- 1 tbsp. Full of honey (optional)
- Diced almonds for topping (optional)

Preparation process

1. Almond milk as well as chia seeds should be combined in a dish. Stir thoroughly.
2. The mixture must be chilled for at least two hrs or overnight for it to thicken.
3. Greek yogurt, mixed berries, as well as chia pudding should be arranged in a glass or dish.
4. Add honey to the top as well as, if preferred, almond dice.
5. Offer cold.

Serving Total

- Kcal:290
- Carbs: 37g
- Fat: 9g
- Protein: 15g

Conclusion

In the fast-paced world of modern cooking, where convenience meets quality, the Air Fryer has emerged as a game-changer, revolutionizing the way we prepare meals. With its advanced technology as well as versatile features, this kitchen appliance has found a put in countless homes, making cooking simpler, more efficient, as well as remarkably enjoyable.

At the heart of the Ninja Air Fryer appeal is its exceptional efficiency. Designed to save both time as well as energy, it offers a wide range of cooking methods, from pressure cooking as well as baking to sautéing as well as steaming, all within a single appliance. Gone are the days of juggling multiple pots as well as pans, as the Air Fryer multifunctionality allows you to create complex dishes with ease.

One of the outstanding features of the Air Fryer is its intelligent cooking programs. With pre-set options for various dishes, it takes the guesswork out of cooking. Whether you're preparing a succulent roast, a creamy risotto, or a batch of fluffy rice, the Air Fryer precision ensures consistently perfect results. This not only saves time but also guarantees that your culinary creations will be met with applause.

The Air Fryer pressure cooking capability deserves special mention. By harnessing the power of pressure, it significantly reduces Cooking Period: s while intensifying flavors. Tough cuts of meat become tender, beans cook to perfection, as well as stews develop deep as well as rich flavors, all in a fraction of the time it would take with traditional methods. It's a culinary breakthrough that has earned the air fryer a devoted following among busy home cooks.

In our fast-paced lives, convenience is paramount. The Air Fryer understands this as well as has been designed with convenience in mind. Its user-friendly interface, clear digital display, as well as easy-to-use controls ensure that even novice chefs can navigate the cooking process effortlessly. The non-stick pot as well as detachable parts make clean-up a breeze, as well as the sleek design adds a touch of modern elegance to any kitchen.

In an era where health-conscious cooking is a top priority, the Air Fryer excels. Its ability to retain nutrients while cooking under pressure ensures that your meals are not only delicious but also wholesome. You can experiment with a wide range of ingredients, from fresh vegetables to lean proteins, as well as know that you're creating meals that nourish both body as well as soul.

Beyond its practicality, the Air Fryer inspires culinary creativity. It encourages you to step out of your comfort zone as well as experiment with new recipes as well as flavors. The Air Fryer versatility means you can try various cuisines from around the world, from hearty Indian curries to delicate French pastries, all within the confines of your own kitchen.

In conclusion, the Air Fryer has become more than just another kitchen appliance; it's a culinary companion that simplifies your cooking experience, enhances your culinary skills, as well as elevates your everyday meals to gourmet status. Whether you're a seasoned chef or a novice cook, the Ninja air fryer welcomes you into a world of culinary delight.

With its efficiency, precision, as well as convenience, the Air Fryer has undoubtedly earned its put in the modern kitchen. It has redefined the way we approach cooking, making it not just a necessity but a true pleasure. As it continues to evolve as well as inspire, it promises to be a kitchen staple for years to come, serving up delicious as well as memorable meals with every use.

Printed in Great Britain
by Amazon